JN452308

Paleolithic Age in Korea

by Kidong BAE

Paleolithic Age in Korea

by Kidong BAE

Paleolithic Age in Korea

PUBLISHED BY Hakyoun Publishing Company
#B-712, Woolim Lion's Valley, 371-28,
Gasan-dong, Geumcheon-ku, Seoul, Korea

First published 29 June 2012

Paleolithic Age in Korea
Publisher 권혁재

Writer Kidong BAE
bkd5374@gmail.om
Editer Kidong BAE and The Institute of Cultural Properties, Hanyang University
www.hyicp.or.kr

Designer Kiryong KIM

ISBN 978-89-5508-283-8 93910

Contents

Prologue

Environment and Culture of Paleolithic Age in Korea

1. Environment and Geology in Korea 11
2. Korean Paleolithic Archaeology Today; a new perspective for 21st century 21
3. Peopling in the Korean Peninsula 37
4. Old artifacts in new contexts: Conservatism? Or Transfomation? 59

Early/Middle Paleolithic Age

5. Patterns of Early Paleolithic in the Korean Peninsula 69
6. History of Handaxe Studies in Korea 83
7. The Movius Line sensu lato (Norton et al., 2006) further assessed and defined 91
8. Middle Pleistocene handaxes from the Korean Peninsula .. 101

Upper Paleolithic Age

9. Origin and patterns of the Upper Paleolithic industries in the Korean Peninsula and movement of modern humans in East Asia 123
10. The nature of the Early to Late Paleolithic transition in Korea: Current perspectives 147
11. A review of Korean Microlithic Industries 177

References

Prologue

The objective of this book is to introduce some important archaeological evidence found in the Korean peninsula up to 2012 and also to explain some of the patterns observed in the archaeological evidence. Topics dealt in this book were selected from most current issues in Korean Paleolithic archaeology from the earliest to the latest stage of the Paleolithic Age in the peninsula. Although it may not be comprehensive introductory book of the Paleolithic archaeology of the peninsula, I hope it may serve as a basic source for Paleolithic archaeology done in Korean peninsula during the last decades.

It has been more than a half century since the first Paleolithic evidence was identified at the Seokjangni site in early 1960s in South Korea. In the recent decades, a great number of Paleolithic localities were found in the southern part of the Korean peninsula owing to numerous salvage archaeological excavations for social development, and more than half were investigated with different intensity. At present, it is very clear on the basis of archaeological evidence found so far that the early hominines dispersed into the Korean peninsula during Middle Pleistocene. Although there are some clear different phases and mixture of cultural patterns in the peninsula from the adjacent areas, the general evolutionary pattern of the Paleolithic industries of the Korean peninsula are not so different from those in the adjacent areas, particular in China.

In spite of the dramatic increase of archaeological data in

the last decades, not many attempts have been made for the explanation of general patterns of stone industries and hominine's adaptive processes on the peninsula. There are some explanations of origin of certain types of stone tool, such as tang point and bifacial points, in Far Eastern Asia. However, most of these are tentative conclusions derived from preliminary observations, so it should be examined with more concrete evidence for explaining some of the patterns in this region. Furthermore, it is more difficult to understand on-site activities at Paleolithic sites except for some late Upper Paleolithic sites, due to the heavy transformation of geo-archaeological contexts.

Patterns of the Paleolithic industries in East Asia, China, Japan, Manchuria, eastern Siberia and Korean peninsula show some similarities and discontinuities of these similarities with local variation of tool types and assemblages. It is believed that the early Homo was dispersed from the southern part of East Asia because it is quite unlikely they moved from Siberia to East Asia because of the unfavorable climate that they could not have had any reliable means to adapt. However, Homo sapiens are considered to have dispersed via two routes to East Asia: North and South routes. Human dispersal into far eastern asia is observed more clear from two direction in north and south in late upper pleistocene while it was obscure due to few supporting evidence for hominine movement in unfavorable environment of eastern siberia. More extensive survey in this region is expected to provide evidence supporting northern movement before upper paleolithic.

The distinct difference in stone industries between the northern and southern parts of East Asia during the Upper Paleolithic can be considered to have resulted from these two movements of Homo sapiens. Considering the overall patterns of the stone industries in this region, the Paleolithic industries in the Korean peninsula are a mixture of different traditions from the North and South. It is somewhat different from the pattern in China, where a clear boundary can be seen in stone industries in Upper Paleolithic.

The most critical problem of Paleolithic archaeology in Korea is to build up an undisputable chronology of stone industries. In recent years, many different chronometric dating methods have been extensively applied; however, it is still far from a clear view of the chronology. There are variations in results when different dating methods are applied and in some cases reversal orders are also observed. In addition, the chronological system of three sub-stages does not represent well the conventional characters of the stone tool technology through time. No development of preparatory technique for flaking makes it very difficult to understand the evolutionary stages of particular stone industries.

Another problem is the different terminologies used by archaeologists who come from different educational backgrounds. Due to a lack of clear definition of nomenclature in many articles and reports, it is very unproductive for a comparative analysis of stone industries from different sites due to confusions in definition. It should be also noted that too much attention is given to stone artefacts researches to typological analysis while few have been done for comparative analysis of technological processes of flaking from core, the so-called debitage process. It may be difficult to carry out these analyses because very few conjoined pieces have been found at most sites. Considering the few distinctive tool types except handaxes and tang points, etc., and many types of cores including polyhedral, flake was probably the most common for direct use for certain purposes. In this sense, flaking technology should be extensively pursued along with typological studies.

In addition to topics in this book, several important issues in Paleolithic archaeology in Korea include the transition to Holocene adaptation from the terminal Paleolithic and post-depositional transformation of sites which would be very critical in understanding early Paleolithic Korea. Understanding the subsistence has been hardly possible because there is very little relevant archaeological evidence that can be found only at a few cave sites. Nevertheless, it needs some elaborate methodology of landscape archaeology in the future.

I owe Kim, Kiryong, my sincere graduate student, who assisted me in completing and editing the original articles. All errors in the text are my responsibility and will be corrected in the future. And I appreciate Mr. Kwon, Hyukje, the publisher, for his kind cooperation in publishing a book in English, which may not be popular in Korea. I wish very much that this book may help foreign researchers to understand the current knowledge of Korean Paleolithic archaeology for criticism as well as general discussion.

Environment and Culture of Paleolithic Age in Korea

CHAPTER 1

Environment and Geology in Korea

Land and Geology

The Korean Peninsula extends out from Manchuria and is surrounded by the Eastern Sea (Japan Sea), the Eastern China Sea, and the Yellow Sea. The geomorphology of the peninsula is characterized by its hilly and mountainous topography(Firgrue 1-1). Approximately two thirds of the land is mountain and low hills. In the western part of the peninsula, relatively flat alluvial plains and a landscape of gently rolling small hills extend

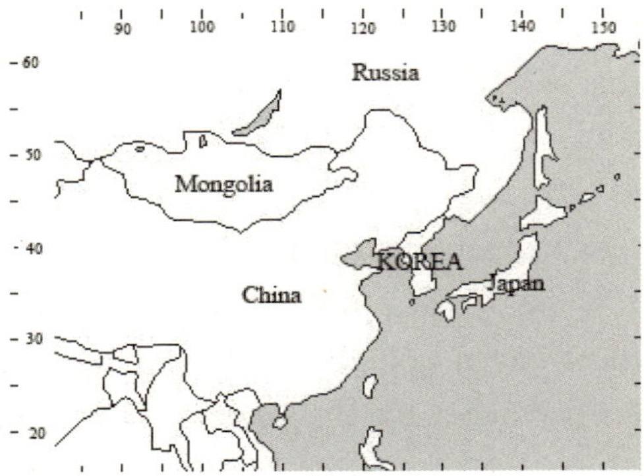

Firgure 1-1. Location of Korean Peninsula

along the western coastline, but high mountain range are distributed in the eastern and northeastern part of the peninsula. The Taebaek backbone mountain range runs south and north along the east in coast. The Taebaek mountain range forms a gentle slope on its western side, but has very steep escarpments on the eastern slopes facing very narrow coastal plains along the Eastern Sea (Japan Sea). The Taebaek mountain range merges into the Gaema high plateau in the north, which is about 1,500 m above sea level. Most of the mountain systems in the western part of the peninsula originate from the Taebaek mountains and the Nangrim mountain range, another backbone mountain in the north, and parallel in a northeast-southwest direction. The mountain is not generally high, although some of the peaks are higher than 1,000 m. However, as the mountains are found all over the peninsula except on the narrow coastal plain along the western coast, the terran is rugged. Accordingly, most of the rivers in the peninsula flow to the west with a low gradient, to the Yellow Sea between these mountain ranges.

It has been thought that the physical differences between the eastern and the western part of the Korean peninsula have been caused by the crustal movements. Geomorphological evidence indicates that the eastern limb had moved upward; on the other hand, the western limp had continued to warp downward (Kobayashi 1953). According to Rustanovich's study, the eastern seaboard was uplifted to about 1,500 m during the Pliocene and the Quarternary, while the western part was submerged during the Quarternary (Rustanovich

1961). The fact that no Pleistocene deposits have been found on the western coast may indicate that the process of tilting continues to the present (Lee 1985).

Climate

The present climate of Korea is defined as temperate with four dominant seasons. In general, summer is very hot and humid while winter is dry and cold. It is relatively mild and warm during spring and fall. The climate of the Korean peninsula is under strong influence from the East Asia Monsoon system. The high pressures formed over the huge land mass of Siberia during the winter bring dry and cold wind to the peninsula and the summer monsoon from the northern Pacific brings abundant moisture and yields high precipitation. The hot and very humid weather during the summer produced by the northern Pacific air mass results in a kind of tropical or sub-tropical climate.

In spite of a few snow falls, three quarters of the total annual precipitation is concentrated in summer from June to September. Especially typhoons from the northern Pacific and cyclones from the Yangtzi river area during the summer period accompany heavy rainfalls. The annual precipitation is fairly high, up to 1,400 or 1,500 ㎜ in the Southern Sea, but it decreases to 500 ㎜ in the northeastern high land (Park 1986; Figure 1-2).

In general, the annual precipitation is over 1,000 ㎜ in most

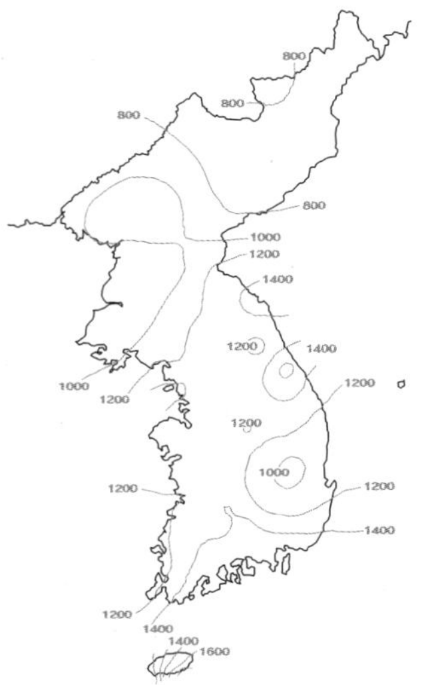

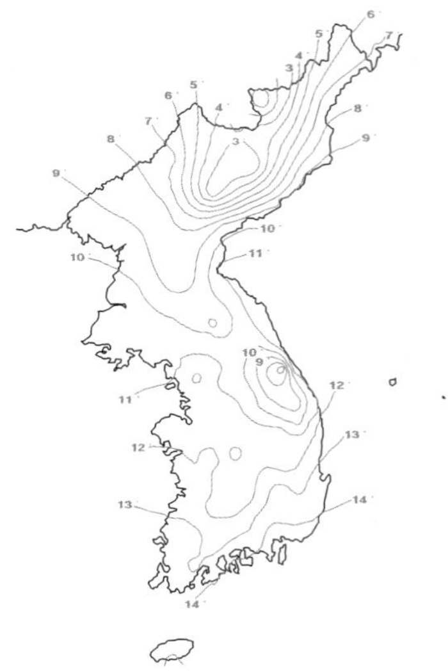

Figure 1-2. Map of annual average rainfall in Korean

Figure 1-3. Map of annual average temperature in Korean

of the peninsula except the northeastern part and several inland areas of the Kyeongsang province in the southeast. The adjacent area of the Chugaryeong Rift Valley, which is the catchment area of the Hantan river, is an area of high precipitation. In Unchon, about 20 ㎞ east of the Chongokni, annual precipitation is recorded up to 1,400 ㎜. The moisture brought from the Yellow Sea becomes rainfall when it rises in front of the high mountains in this area.

The range of the annual mean temperature falls between 15 ℃ and 3 ℃ (Figure 1-3). The lowest annual mean temperature is recorded in the northeastern high land. I genneral, the annual difference of temperature in the northeastern highland is much greater than the difference in the southern part of the peninsula. During the summer, the difference in temperature between the northern high land and the Jeju island in the south is not so great, about 8 ℃ (26 ℃ in the Jeju island and 18 ℃ in the northeastern high land), however, the mean temperature differs 24 ℃ between the too extreme areas. In the northern area, spring and fall seasons are relatively short, while in the southern part these seasons are longer.

Flora

The present vegetation of the Korean peninsula is dominated by various temperate species. The varied climate results in a diversity of plant species, believed to be much richer than any other place in the same latitude in the world (Lee 1982). The Korean peninsula is often divided into three vegetation types on the basis of the forest types: Warm Temperate Vegetation, Temperate Vegetation, and Cold Temperate Vegetation (Figure 1-4). As the Temperate Vegetation covers most of the peninsula, it is often divided into several sub-areas. These forest types show a zonal distribution parallel with the latitude. The mountainous landscape of the peninsula creates another type of zonal distribution of plant species along with altitude change.

Broad leaved evergreen forest grow a on the Warm Temperate Vegetation areas which are the southern coastal areas of the peninsula, including the lowland of the Jeju island where the climate is characterized by high precipitation and warm temperature (mean annual temperature, about 14 ℃). In

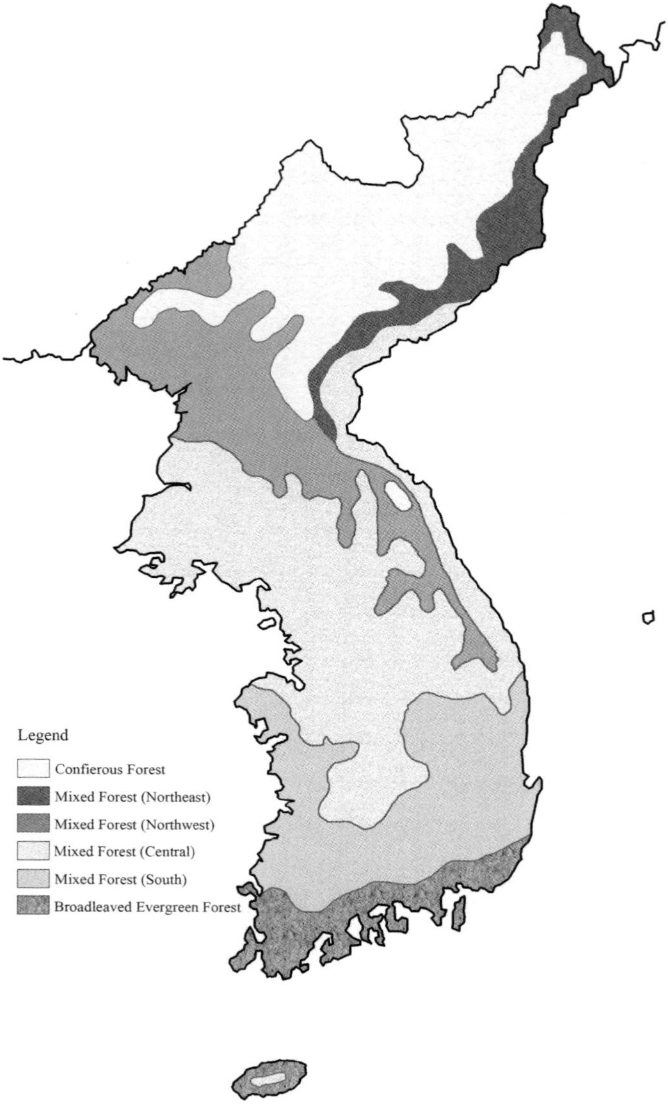

Figure 1-4. Vegetation zones of Korea

these areas, *Cyclobalanopsis auia, Cinnamomum camphora, machilus rimosa var. thunbergii, Camellia japonica, Castanopsis cusoidata var. siebodic and Masakia japonica, etc.* are dominant species in the woodland. These species decrease gradually moving inland from the coastline and are replaced by a deciduous broaleaved forest.

Most of the Korean peninsula is covered by Temperate Vegetaion. Deciduous broadleaf forest covers most of the lowland of the peninsula except the southern coastline, Jeju island, and the northeastern highland. *Zelkova sezata, Celtis willdenowiana, Carpinus laxiflora, Pinus thunbergina* and *phyllostach reticulata* represent species derived from warm temperate deciduous broaleaf forest, while *Quercus mongolia, Quercus dentata, Quercus acutissima* and *Castanea crenata* increase in the north. In the of tree species in the forest gradually changes as in one moves towards the north. In the same type of forest in Japan, *Fagus multinerus* is a common species, but this species is confined to the Ulneung island in the Eastern Sea. It cannot grow in the peninsula, probably become of the high temperature in summer and low temperature of the soil (Kim 1976).

Cold temperate vegetation covers the northeastern area high mountains in the Korean peninsula. Annual mean temperature is lower than 10 ℃ in the northeastern high land area and about 10 ℃ in the high mountain part in the middle of the Korean peninsula. An evergreen coniferous forest is present in the areas of the Cold Temperate Vegetation. The evergreen forest includes trees like *Picea jezonensis, Abies nephrolepis,*

Abies koreana, Pinus pumila, Larix olgensis, and Alnus japonica, etc. In the relatively mild area of the Cold Temperate Vegetation, broadleaf deciduous trees like *Alnus japonica, Populus maxinowiczii, Quercus mongolica, Quercus dentata, Chosenaoa bracteosa, Betula platyphylla, Betula ermanii, Salix myrtilloides,* and *Vaccinum ulginosum,* etc., are mixed with the coniferous species. These species grow especially in wet areas and near creeks where coniferous trees cannot grow well. Going up to a high altitude close to the alpine zone, some species of *Beltula* are dominant in the Cold Temperate Vegetation and Pinus pumila represent in the lower part of alpine zone. The upper part of the alpine zone is covered with grassland. Sub-alpine flora is found in the southern part of Korea, however alpine forest appears at 1,000 m above sea level on Mt. Baekdu which is located at 42° N in the northeastern part of Korea. Many species living in this area are also found in Manchuria where the climate is similar.

Mammalian Fauna

Korea is located near the southern boundary of the Palaeoarcitc mammalian region. In the northeastern high, cold adapted animals are found, while some sub-tropical species also exist in the southern coastal area including Jeju island. However, temperate represent the general characteristic of the fauna in the Korean Peninsula. Most of the animal species found in Korea are common on the Asian continent, while endemic species are very few. The mammalian species currently living in the Korean peninsula represent 7 orders, 25 families, 63 genera, and 165 species (Kim et al. 1978).

Zoogeography of the Korean peninsula can be divided into two region: Siberian sub-region and the Chinese (Manchurian) sub-region. The northeastern highland of the Korean peninsula is a part of the Siberian sub-region. The animals in the region are represented by *Cervus elaphus, Capreolus capreolus, Panthera tigris altaica, Naemorhedus goral raddenanus, Manchuian weasel, Martes flavigula koreana, Cervus nippon, Korthulorum, Ursus arctors* and *Felis lynx,* etc. The composition of animal species of this area shows very close affinities to those of northern Manchuria, Sakhalin, and Hokkaido. The rest of area in the Korean peninsula belong to the Chinese sub-region is relatively milder than that of the Siverian sub-region. The animal species living in this area include *Talpa micrura coreana, Lepus sinensis coreanus, Canis lupus, vulpes peculiosa, Selenarctos thibetanus, Panthera pardus orientalis, Felis silvestris,* and *Hydropotes inermis,* etc. A few endemic species and subspecies of small animals such as bat and rat are found in each region.

CHAPTER 2

Korean Paleolithic Archaeology Today; a new perspective for 21st century

Introduction

In the last half century, a great deal of Paleolithic researches have been carried out and enormous amount of Paleolithic data has been formed for studies of human evolution in the Korean peninsula and adjacent areas. Especially, many significant advances have been achieved from archaeological excavations and discussions at international seminars. However, critical questions remain to be solved in future researches with collaboration of other sciences and international archaeologists. Major concerns of Paleolithic archaeology in Korea at present time are explanation of evolutionary process of stone industries with relatively accurate chronology and reconstruction of hominine behavior, which could be inferred from contexts of stone artefact assemblages. Except stone industries of late

Upper Pleistocene, both of the topics are far from being explained with some clear visions due to lack of rigorous attempts to pursue these issues with reasonable methodologies.

Development in the last decade of the 21st century

Numerous sites have been excavated through salvage archaeology all over the Korean peninsula (Figure 2-1). New local regions have been added for Paleolithic finds and Paleolithic information of a local area or a basin has become richer and richer by researches in the past decade. Longer sequence of Paleolithic industries in a local region has been developed as well. Significant development of scientific analysis has been achieved from international collaboration researches in some regions, for example HIRB (Hantan-Imjin river basin) and the Mansuri sites (e. g. Yi et al., 2005, Lee et al. 2006, Bae et al. 2008, Matsufuji 2008). These scientific researches made a great advance in our understanding of geology and environment as well as transformation processes of sites. Plenty of occasions have been offered for discussions about current results from newly done researches as well as existing patterns of Paleolithic industries at domestic and international gatherings of Paleolithic archaeologists and international scientists in Korea and abroad, such as APA(*Asian Paleolithic Association*) meetings. A great deal of development has been made in Paleolithic archaeological information and explanations of patterns of Paleolithic culture for understanding past hominines' behavior in the last decades of the 21st century.

Figure 2-1. Excavated sites of South Korea in the 21st century

Chronology and Age Dates

Three sub-age system of Paleolithic Age is common in archaeology books in East Asia, however in some professional papers of Paleolithic archaeology new attempts of chronology of Paleolithic Age in regions have appeared in different frameworks. Several different sub-stages have been offered by some archaeologists in Korea (Yi 2000, Lee 2004, Sung 2004), but the most critical chronological system comparing to the conventional chronological system is the two sub-ages, Lower or Early, and Upper Paleolithic without sub-stage of Middle Paleolithic (Bae 2006; 2009). It has been a critical topic whether 'Middle Paleolithic' is relevant for the Paleolithic chronology in East Asia or not, because no true Levallois technique appeared in this area (Lycett 2007), and no technological change in flake making has been observed. In addition, no clear tendency appeared in making small tools in stone artefact assemblages prior to the appearance of blade technology.

"Middle Paleolithic" is often used for some stone industries which look crude and are considered of age between 100,000 BP and 35,000 BP. Even an age of between 200,000 BP and 35,000 BP has been used for "Middle Paleolithic" in Korea (Lee 2002; 2004), which is probably based on the age of the first appearance of Levallois in Europe. Because stone industries before the presence of blade technology are hardly distinguishable in debitage technology and variation in stone tool assemblages, it is not relevant to make sub-stages in these type of stone industries.

In the 21st century, many age dates of Paleolithic industries obtained from various scientific analyses have been accumulated (Table 2-1, Figure 2-2); OSL, tephra, K/Ar, AMS, ^{26}Al-^{10}Be, etc. Most of OSL dates remain within the last 100,000 years except some results from sites in the HIRB. Some OSL dates obtained from a single site, for example

Table 2-1. Chronometric dates of Lower Paleolithic sites in 21st century, Korea.

Site Name	Layer	Age	Methods	Reference
Chongokni	Layer Ⅴ	31,500 ± 600 BP	AMS	Vasilchuk et al. (2002)
		31,000 ± 600 BP		
		35,700 ± 3000 BP		
	Layer Ⅱ	59,000 ± 2,000 BP	OSL	Naruse et al. (2003)
	Layer Ⅷ	123,000 ± 8,000 BP		
	Layer Ⅸ	>160,000 BP		
	Layer Ⅸ	>200,000 BP	TT-OSL	Kim et al. (2008)
	Layer Ⅵ	417,000 ± 87,000 BP	^{26}Al-^{10}Be	Lebatard (2011)
	Layer Ⅸ	830,000 ± 102,000 BP		
	Layer Ⅺ	652,000 ± 92,000 BP		
	Layer Ⅺ	492,000 ± 81,000 BP		
Kawoli	Layer Ⅳ	47,000 ± 11,000 BP	IRSL	Nagatomo (2005)
	Layer Ⅳ	51,000 ± 23,000 BP		
	Layer Ⅴ	78,000 ± 24,000 BP		
Wondang Jangnamgyo	Layer Ⅷ	325,000 ± 137,000 BP	^{26}Al-^{10}Be	Lebatard (2011)
	Layer Ⅴ	393,000 ± 137,000 BP	^{26}Al-^{10}Be	
	Layer Ⅵ	454,000 ± 94,000 BP	^{26}Al-^{10}Be	
Keumpari	Layer 3	30,800 ± 100 BP	AMS	Bae et al. (2006)
		31,400 ± 400 BP	AMS	
		31,500 ± 1300 BP	AMS	
	Layer 5	45,000 ± 7,000 BP	IRSL	Nagatomo (2005)
Jangsanri	Silt Layer	206,000 ± 21,000 BP	IRSL	Nagatomo (2005)
		220,000 ± 26,000 BP	IRSL	
		215,000 ± 41,000 BP	IRSL	
	Sediment	90,000 ± 7,000 BP	OSL	Kim & Hong (2004)
		103,000 ± 7,000 BP	OSL	
		97,000 ± 8,000 BP	OSL	
		105,000 ± 10,000 BP	OSL	
Unjung	Culture 1	35,000 ± 3000 BP	OSL	Lee et al. (2009)
		37,000 ± 3000 BP	OSL	
		39,000 ± 2000 BP	OSL	

		44,000 ± 3000 BP	OSL	
		45,000 ± 3000 BP	OSL	
Janggi	Cultural Layer 1	48,000 ± 3,300 BP	OSL	Jeon (2008)
	Cultural Layer 2	30,800 ± 2,600 BP 43,000 ± 3,500 BP > 50,000 BP	OSL AMS AMS	
	Cultural Layer 3	30,200 ± 2,000 BP	OSL	
Yeonyangri	Layer 4	63,000 ± 4,000 BP 67,000 ± 3,000 BP	OSL OSL	Kim & Lee (2005)
Geumsani Galdun	Layer 4	3,800 ± 500 BP	OSL	Choi & Kim (2008)
	Layer 5A	38,000 ± 4,000 BP	OSL	
	Layer 5B	68,000 ± 2,000 BP 30,400 ± 200 BP	OSL AMS	
	Layer 6A	86,000 ± 6,000 BP 29,900 ± 100 BP	OSL AMS	
	Layer 6B	92,000 ± 7,000 BP 98,000 ± 5,000 BP 102,000 ± 9,000 BP 37,300 ± 400 BP 28,000 ± 150 BP	OSL OSL OSL AMS AMS	
Geoduri	Layer 2	28,100 ± 200 BP	AMS	Park & Hong (2009)
	Layer 3	62,000 ± 3,000 BP	OSL	
	Layer 4	57,000 ± 4,300 BP	OSL	
	Layer 6	78,000 ± 4,800 BP	OSL	
	Layer 8	100,000 ± 7,700 BP	OSL	
Gihwari Cave	Cultural Layer	58,000 ± 3,000 BP 29,700 ± 400 BP 28,400 ± 300 BP 34,990 ± 410 BP 39,280 ± 470 BP	OSL AMS AMS AMS AMS	Park (2008)
Jangheungri	Cultural Layer	24,200 ± 600 BP 24,400 ± 600 BP	AMS AMS	Choi et al. (2001)
Mangsangdong Gigok	Cultural Layer 1	10,200 ± 60 BP	AMS	Choi (2003)
	Cultural	32,100 ± 1,100 BP	AMS	

	Layer 2	33,500 ± 1,200 BP	AMS	
		36,070 ± 380 BP	AMS	
Mukhojindong Wolso	Cultural Layer 4	89,000 ± 4,000 BP	OSL	Choi (2003)
		79,000 ± 5,000 BP	OSL	
	Cultural Layer 5	81,000 ± 10,000 BP	OSL	
		96,000 ± 14,000 BP	OSL	
Mansuri	Loc. 4 2a	65,000 + 8,000/-12,000 BP	OSL	Shitaoka et al. (2008)
		76,000 + 8,000/-6,000 BP	OSL	
	Loc. 4 2b	75,000 + 22,000/-14,000 BP	OSL	
		84,000 + 2,000/-4,000 BP	OSL	
	Loc. 4 2c	104,000 + 2,000/-4,000 BP	OSL	
		115,000 + 10,000/-15,000 BP	OSL	
	Loc. 4 5c	481,000 ± 152,000 BP	^{26}Al-^{10}Be	Lebatard (2011)
		407,000 ± 118,000 BP	^{26}Al-^{10}Be	
		261,000 ± 104,000 BP	^{26}Al-^{10}Be	
		558,000 ± 116,000 BP	^{26}Al-^{10}Be	
		714,000 ± 113,000 BP	^{26}Al-^{10}Be	
		714,000 ± 84,000 BP	^{26}Al-^{10}Be	
	Loc. 1 Layer 5	50,000 ± 3,000 BP	OSL	Park (2010)
		51,000 ± 4,000 BP	OSL	
		92,000 ± 3,000 BP	OSL	
		104,000 ± 7,000 BP	OSL	
	Loc. 1 Layer 6	53,000 ± 3,000 BP	OSL	
		52,000 ± 4,000 BP	OSL	
		95,000 ± 4,000 BP	OSL	
	Loc. 1 Layer 7	44,000 ± 4,000 BP	OSL	
	Loc. 1 Layer 10	103,000 ± 8,000 BP	OSL	
	Loc. 1 Layer 12(send)	44,000 ± 4,000 BP	OSL	
		49,000 ± 4,000 BP	OSL	
		49,000 ± 3,000 BP	OSL	
		68,000 ± 4,000 BP	OSL	
Jangdongri	Layer 3	81,000 ± 2,000 BP	OSL	Kim (2003)
	Layer 6	98,000 ± 3,000 BP	OSL	
	Layer 9	134,000 ± 4,000 BP	OSL	
	Layer 10	137,000 ± 3,000 BP	OSL	

	Layer 11	148,000 ± 6,000 BP	OSL	
	Layer 13	225,000 ± 6,000 BP	OSL	
	Layer 14	156,000 ± 6,000 BP	OSL	
	Layer 18	194,000 ± 11,000 BP	OSL	
	Layer 21	187,000 ± 5,000 BP	OSL	
	Layer 22	193,000 ± 6,000 BP	OSL	
Chungokri	Layer 4	45,000 ± 3,000 BP	OSL	Lee (2006)
	Layer 5	75,000 ± 7,000 BP	OSL	
		78,000 ± 4,000 BP	OSL	

those from the Mansuri site (Shitaoka et al. 2008, Park 2007), do not confirm the order of the sediments; an age date from the upper part of the sediment is older than the lower. New application of cosmic ray method, $^{26}Al-^{10}Be$ method, produced quite older results than results from any other dating method (Lebatard 2011) although it is believed one of the fantastic discovery of dating science in archaeology because all and any stone fascinating can be dated. In case of the sites in the Hantan river basin, Much younger dates of AMS dates obtained from charcoal are claimed to represent the age of stone industries in this area (Yi 2010) which have been considered much older dates on the basis of many other scientific methods. In spite of all efforts for building up a reliable chronology of the Korean Paleolithic stone industries, it is still far from the ultimate goal, although these dates have been used for explanation of chronology of certain particular industries in the peninsula by individual archaeologists. It may need much more rigorous and extensive comparative researches with new perspectives of existing archaeological data.

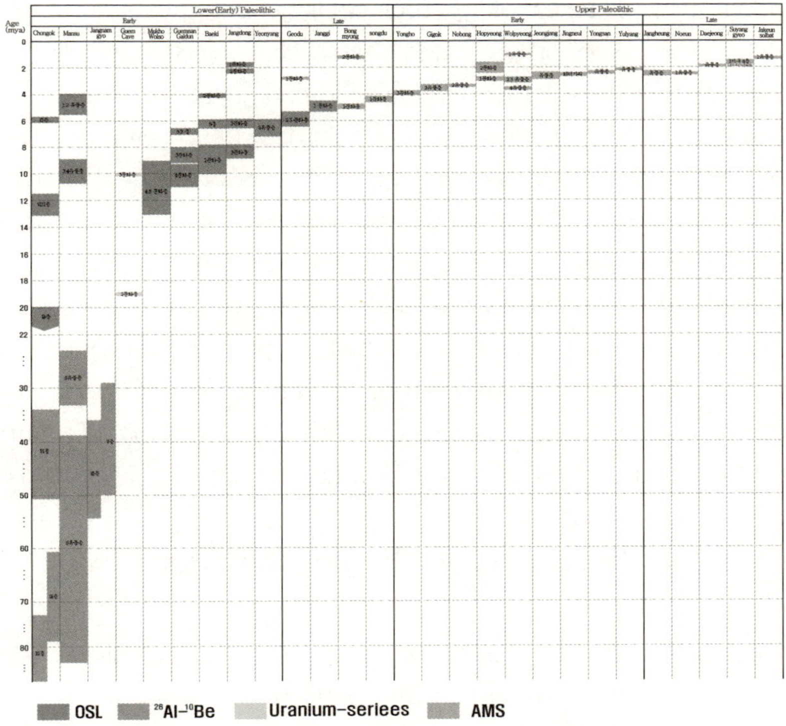

Figure 2-2. Chronometric dates of Primary Paleolithic sites

Classification and Terminology

At present, the National Institute of Cultural Properties in Korea is editing a new dictionary of Paleolithic archaeology in Korea. In this dictionary, most of nomenclature in Paleolithic archaeology in Korea will be included with some definition including some different Korean version of a single term in western language. Lots of variations can be found in individual use of terminology and classification systems (Sohn 1972, Jeong 1976; 1978, Park 1983, Bae 1988) invented in western World, Clark and Kleindinst system (Clark & Kleindienst 1974), Bordes system (Bordes 1981), etc. In some cases, it is not certain whether identification of particular arte-fact is relevant to the applied term. At present, it is very dif-ficult to understand specific character of stone artefacts and assemblages for comparative analyses. It would be necessary to create a new system of terminology and classification, which are relevant to description of properties of stone in-dustries in the Korean peninsula with consideration of com-parative researches with those in adjacent areas.

Paleolithic Traditions vs Regional Pattern

"Tradition" is often referred in many texts of Paleolithic ar-chaeology to describe a certain pattern of stone industries, even early Paleolithic, in East Asia. For example '*Chopper-chopping tool tradition*' is one of the most used term for explaining crude appearance of stone industries in East Asia (Movius 1944; 1948). In China, two traditions of '*Large Tri-hedral Point tradition*' and '*Small Tool Tradition*' are of-ten mentioned even in present papers to synthesis of overall pattern of particular industry (Huang 1989; 1994, Olsen 2009).

In early Paleolithic in the Korean peninsula, so called 'han-daxe tradition' has been observed as a characteristic tool making. At present, more than 20 sites, mostly in central part of the peninsula, were reported certain types of handaxes, whether elaborated forms or crude forms (Figure 2-3). It is now a general understanding that handaxe making is one of pattern in tool making of early Paleolithic whether it is found or not. Another common pattern in early stone industries is presence of many different types of polyhedral shapes in

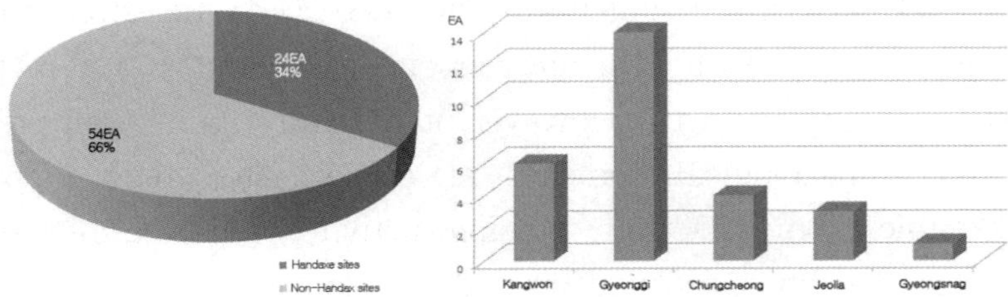

Figure 2-3. Rate of excavated handaxes and quantity of handaxes by the regions

industries. This is much more common than handaxe in early Paleolithic industries although it is present in some Upper Paleolithic industries in the peninsula. Crude forms of handaxes with large flake scars on surface and polyhedral of many different stages of reduction could be considered a tool assemblage representing heavy reliance on flakes as tools without extensive modification. It would be supported by few pieces of secondary retouches and retouches by few and simple retouches for edge modification even on retouched pieces. It would be more appropriate to refer early Paleolithic industries in the Korean peninsula as 'primary-flake tool tradition' although handaxes make a strong impression to archaeologists and other ordinary people.

Stone industries prior to the presence of micro-blade are often found in relatively consolidated sediments below the cultural layer of micro-blade near the present surface. At many localities of Upper Paleolithic after the appearance of micro-blade technology, concentration of artefacts and features on a single horizon, floor, are often present and provide some evidence of activities at each site. For example the Haga site (Lee 2008, 2011), the Jingeuneul site (Lee 2004), the stone tool making atelier at the Suyanggae site (Lee and Kong 2003; 2006) ect. (Figure 2-4). However, it is hardly found well preserved archaeological contexts at earlier sites than Upper Paleolithic, from which any hominin activites could be inferred. In many localities, isolated artefacts or loosely associated assemblages are more common in transformed contexts of colluviums. Even in fine sediments such as loess, poor concentrations of artefacts were often exposed even though density may be a little higher than other part of a site. It is generally believed that most of Paleolithic sites before Upper Paleolithic Age have experienced various post depositional transformations in the process of sedimentation to current loci if they cannot be explained remnants of intentional disposal at the site.

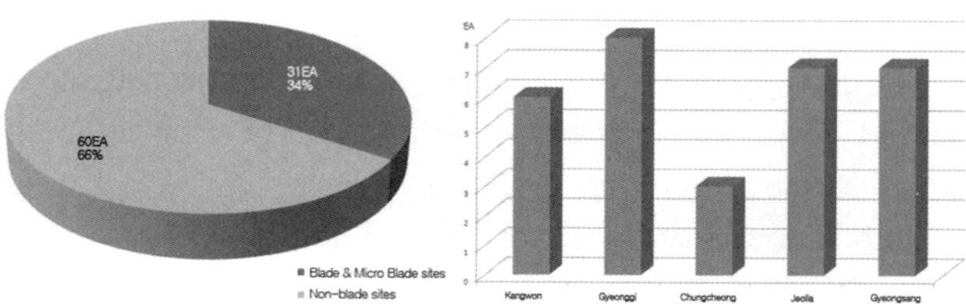

Figure 2-4. Rate of excavated Blade & Micro Blade and quantity of Blade by the regions

In the excavations in 21st century, artefacts were found in concentrated gravels by winnowing processes at the bottom of sediments of many localities in the lower reach of the Han river [e.g. Singok and Janggi site (Jeon 2010; 2011)]. Similar archaeo-geological contexts were exposed at the Songduri site (Lee 2006) and the Dangga site (Lee et al. 2004) previously. It is very evident that these assemblages have experienced very heavy transformation from the original contexts which would have disappeared long time before the final deposition at present localities as contexts explained. It would be very difficult to estimate the age of the stone artefacts assemblages and even the mixture of different stone industries, and furthermore the age of the site. In fact, some stone artefacts found in this kind of context were apparently curate couple of times with long intervals which are assumed by the difference of wear pattern of flake scars on each artefact. It is often remarked the age of the stone industries from this type of contexts on the basis of the age of the sediment, but it is quite unlikely, possibly much older age than the age of the present sediments (Bae 2000). It would be very helpful to do some experimental approaches and active a geological observation at present contexts for understanding processes and age of such accumulations.

New Approach to Upper Paleolithic Archaeology

As in the other part of the World, Upper Paleolithic in Korea is the one of the most interesting and dynamic field of archaeology due to rich its archaeological data. The number of sites and industries has been increased rapidly and well preserved archaeological contexts enable much more interesting explanations of hominine behavior in environment in the Korean peninsula. Also, they provide relevant data for comparative researches in a wide region including Japanese archipelago, Manchuria and northern East Asia. In fact, there are wonderful observations and explanations of tang points and microlithic patterns on the basis of core shapes by international archaeologists as well as Korean archaeologists. Recently, the bifacial points from the Haga site and other localities have been compared to those of similar types found in Japanese archipelago (Lee 2007; 2008). There are different views on how tang points were originated in Korea and diffused to adjacent areas (Lee 2004, Jang 2007). At any rate, these different types of pointed tools from the Upper Paleolithic along with microlithic industries for composite tools were evidently used for hunting gears, especially efficient in hunting large fauna prevailed in this age. Recently, mammoth tooth was found in southwestern part of Korean peninsula, which may be informative in understanding expansion of these tool types into peninsula.

One of the most crucial approaches of the Upper Paleolithic archaeology is collaboration studies of genetics of modern population in this region. Genetic data become rich in modern days not only for modern population and archaeological human remains as well. These new data would be indispensable to

Table 2-2. Stone industry in Korea

Lower (Early) Paleolithic	Early	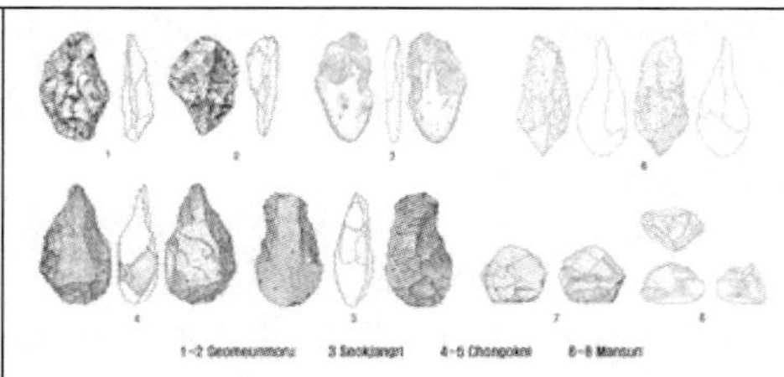
	Late	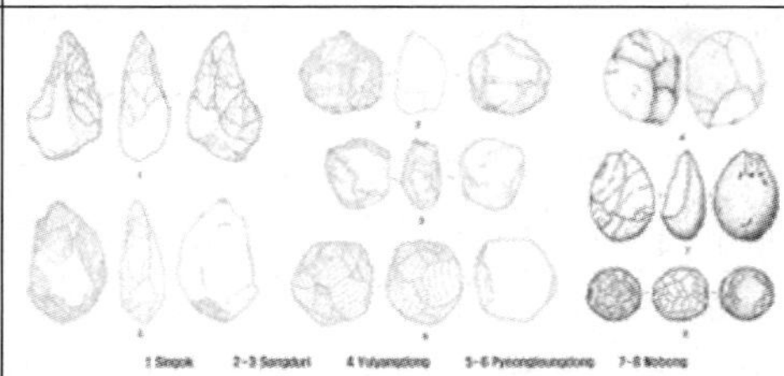
Upper Paleolithic	Early	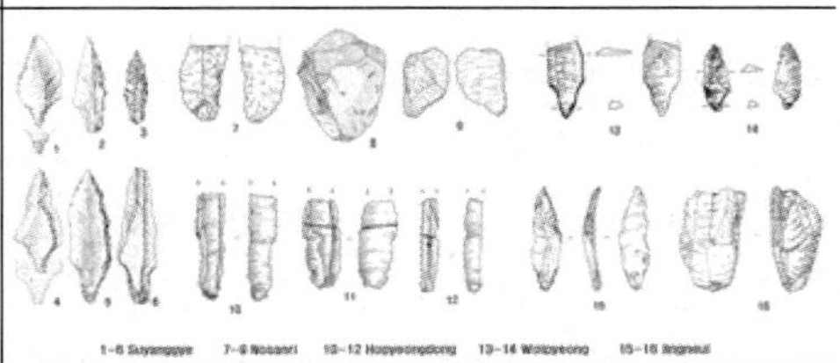
	Late	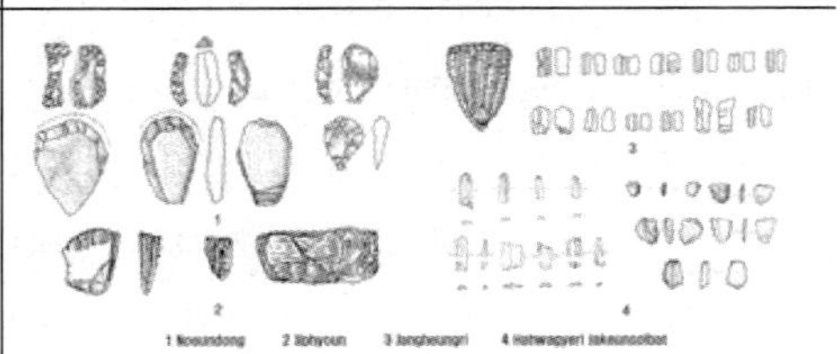

understand population pattern and cultural changes during the Upper Paleolithic in this region. The North-South hypothesis of human dispersal into the Far Eastern Asia including the Korean peninsula would be one of the most interesting approaches to the patterns of Upper Paleolithic in the region (Omoto & Saitou 1997, Bannai et al. 2007, Naruya 2008, Bae

2010). This model would be helpful to understand the general pattern of stone industries in East Asia including bifaces.

Conclusion

Although data of Paleolithic industries have been expanded very rapidly in the last couple of decades in the Korean peninsula in terms of quantity and quality of stone tool industries and results from scientific analysis, lots of questions in understanding patterns remain unsolved and some new questions have been added. It is regrettable that we have done lots of excavations at many important localities but few discussions for interpretations on the basis of extensive and intensive observations of patterns of Paleolithic data that we have had.

Now, the number of excavations for salvage archaeology has been decreased recently. It is pity for Korean archaeologists, but it could provide some rooms for returning ourselves to making good observations and constructing potential hypothesis for better explanations. In doing these efforts, we may need much more advanced methodology and collaboration with related sciences, especially science of dating. Activating observation and experimental approach to site transformation would be essential part of development of methodologies. Building up classification system and nomenclature with clear definition and wide application would be pre-liquisite and indispensible part in development of advancement of methodology for the Paleolithic archaeology in Korea.

CHAPTER 3

Peopling in the Korean Peninsula

Introduction

Current evidence from China indicates that initial hominin occupation in northern Asia extends to the Early Pleistocene (~1.6 Ma or older: Zhu et al. 2003). Since the Korean peninsula was never geographically isolated from the Chinese mainland, it has been postulated that the early hominin migrations into northern China could also have extended to the Korean peninsula. However, currently few Early and early Middle Pleistocene sites have been identified in Korea (Norton 2000; Bae 2001). Current Paleolithic research in Korea is focused on the important questions surrounding the circumstances of the earliest peopling of Korea. This research hopes to understand where the earliest migration of hominins onto the Korean peninsula took place and which hominin species is responsible for this migration Due to the acidic soils, which inhibit bone pres-

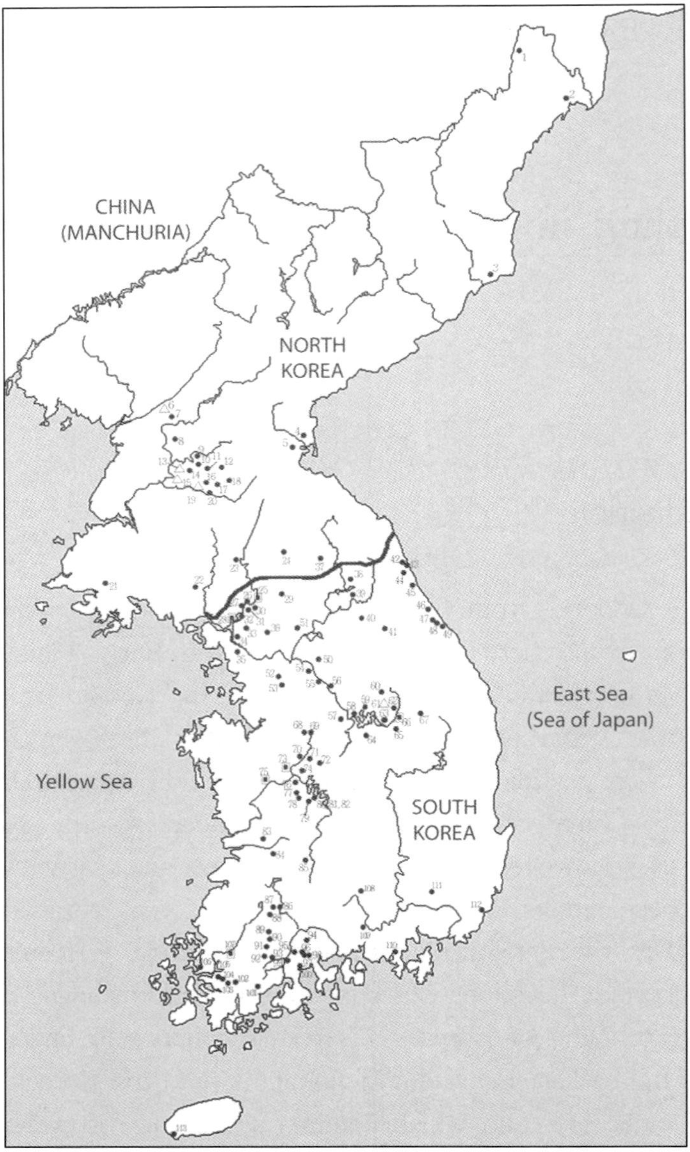

Fig. 3.1 Primary Paleolithic sites from the Korean Peninsula

No.	Sites	Notes	No.	Sites	Notes
1	Dongwanjin	Paleolithic Sites	58	Myeongori	Paleolithic Sites
2	Fulpori	Paleolithic Sites	59	Sagiri	Paleolithic Sites
3	Jangdeongni	Paleolithic Sites	60	Jeommal cave	Paleolithic Sites
4	Dajeonni	Paleolithic Sites	61	Sangsiri	Hominid Fossil Site
5	Guljaedeok	Paleolithic Sites	62	Gunang cave	Paleolithic Sites
6	Dokchon-seungrisan	Hominid Fossil Site	63	Suyanggae	Paleolithic Sites
7	Punggongni	Paleolithic Sites	64	Sangsi-geuneul	Paleolithic Sites
8	Miljeonni	Paleolithic Sites	65	Dodamni	Paleolithic Sites
9	Geumpyeongni	Paleolithic Sites	66	Keum cave	Earliest Paleolithic Sites
10	Seungho cave	Paleolithic Sites	67	Yeondang Ssang cave	Paleolithic Sites
11	Maeri	Paleolithic Sites	68	Janggwanni	Paleolithic Sites
12	Heungnyeong	Paleolithic Sites	69	Songduri	Paleolithic Sites
13	Mandalri	Hominid Fossil Site	70	Sorori	Paleolithic Sites
14	Hwacheonni	Paleolithic Sites	71	Yulyangdong	Paleolithic Sites
15	Ryokpori	Hominid Fossil Site	72	Durubong	Paleolithic Sites
16	Komonmoru	Paleolithic Sites	73	Mansuri	Earliest Paleolithic Sites
17	Cheonjaeam	Paleolithic Sites	74	Saem cave	Paleolithic Sites
18	Bancheonni	Paleolithic Sites	75	Sokchangni	Earliest Paleolithic Sites
19	Ryonggokni	Hominid Fossil Site	76	Nosanni	Paleolithic Sites
20	Geumcheon cave	Paleolithic Sites	77	Daejeongdong	Paleolithic Sites
21	Daetanni	Paleolithic Sites	78	Gwanpyeongdong	Paleolithic Sites
22	Haesang	Paleolithic Sites	79	Gujeukdong	Paleolithic Sites
23	Hoengsanni	Paleolithic Sites	80	Dunsan	Paleolithic Sites
24	Jangheungni	Paleolithic Sites	81	Yongsandong	Paleolithic Sites
25	Chongokni	Earliest Paleolithic Sites	82	Noeundong	Paleolithic Sites
26	Namgyeri	Paleolithic Sites	83	Sinmak	Paleolithic Sites
27	Wondangni	Paleolithic Sites	84	Sageunni	Paleolithic Sites
28	Jangsanni	Earliest Paleolithic Sites	85	Chimgokni	Paleolithic Sites
29	Hwadaeri Shimteo	Paleolithic Sites	86	Jewolni	Paleolithic Sites
30	Gawolni	Paleolithic Sites	87	Songjeonni	Paleolithic Sites
31	Juwolni	Paleolithic Sites	88	Okgwa	Paleolithic Sites
32	Geumpari	Paleolithic Sites	89	Hwagok	Paleolithic Sites
33	Unjeong	Paleolithic Sites	90	Jukongni	Paleolithic Sites
34	Gawaji	Paleolithic Sites	91	Chipyeongdong	Paleolithic Sites
35	Janggi	Paleolithic Sites	92	Daejeonni	Paleolithic Sites
36	Minrakdong	Paleolithic Sites	93	Juksanni	Paleolithic Sites
37	Geoduri	Paleolithic Sites	94	Juknaeri	Paleolithic Sites
38	Sangmuryongni	Paleolithic Sites	95	Geumcheon cave	Paleolithic Sites
39	Budongni	Paleolithic Sites	96	Usanni Gokcheon	Paleolithic Sites
40	Hahwagyeri	Paleolithic Sites	97	Sinpyeongni	Paleolithic Sites
41	Hyeoncheonni	Paleolithic Sites	98	Wolpyeong	Paleolithic Sites
42	Guhodong	Paleolithic Sites	99	Okcheon	Paleolithic Sites
43	Gumidong	Paleolithic Sites	100	Deoksanni	Paleolithic Sites
44	Jusuri	Paleolithic Sites	101	Sanging	Paleolithic Sites
45	Simgokni	Paleolithic Sites	102	Yongho	Paleolithic Sites
46	Gigok	Paleolithic Sites	103	Dangga, Chongok	Paleolithic Sites
47	Nobong	Paleolithic Sites	104	Dasanni	Paleolithic Sites
48	Balhandong	Paleolithic Sites	105	Piseori	Paleolithic Sites
49	Bukpyeongdong	Paleolithic Sites	106	Danghasan	Paleolithic Sites
50	Andeonkni	Paleolithic Sites	107	Jangdongni	Earliest Paleolithic Sites
51	Hopyeongdong	Paleolithic Sites	108	Imbulri	Paleolithic Sites
52	Pyeongchangni	Paleolithic Sites	109	Naechonni	Paleolithic Sites
53	Samri	Paleolithic Sites	110	Igeumdong	Paleolithic Sites
54	Byeongsanni	Paleolithic Sites	111	Goryeri	Paleolithic Sites
55	Yeonyangni	Paleolithic Sites	112	Haeundae	Paleolithic Sites
56	Keungilga	Paleolithic Sites	113	Gosanri	Paleolithic Sites
57	Ochangri	Paleolithic Sites			

ervation at most open-air sites, stone artifacts are usually the only hominin traces recovered at Pleistocene localities in Korea. Understanding the nature of these lithic technologies is critical to understanding how early hominins adapted to the Korean environment. The focus of this paper is to present an updated review of the Korean paleoanthropological record since Norton's (2000) synthesis.

Most of the northern part of the peninsula has not been intensively investigated for paleoanthropological traces. Some cave sites have yielded hominin fossils and stone industries from the Late Paleolithic. Due to an improved socio-economic situation and a growing interest in paleoanthropology, more than 100 Paleolithic sites have been identified in the southern part of the peninsula (Norton 2000, 2007; Sohn et. al, 2002; Figure 3-1). Since few absolute dates are available and many sites are considered to have been secondarily deposited, it is difficult to construct an absolute chronology for many of these sites and associated materials (Bae 2002a). The age of many of these sites unfortunately falls between the limits of most dating methods. Fortunately, the recent application of tephrochronological studies provides an invaluable methodology for developing a confident chronostratigraphy of Early Paleolithic sites in Korea.

The Oldest Hominin Fossils from the Korean Peninsula

The earliest hominin fossils were excavated from limestone

caves in central South Korea and the Pyoungyang area in North Korea (Norton 2000; Park and Lee, 2004). All of the hominin fossils in South Korea have been dated to the Late Pleistocene. Some hominin fossils found in North Korea are considered to be Middle Pleistocene in age. The North Korean hominin fossil material is discussed here (see Norton 2000 for discussion of the South Korean hominin fossil record; Figure 3-2).

Two molars from Dokchon are considered to be archaic Homo sapiens (Institute of Archaeology 1978). Unfortunately no stone artifacts were found in association with these specimens, and no absolute dates are available for this site. Several fragments of a hominin juvenile male's skull were collected from sediments of Middle Pleistocene age from Daehyundong in Pyoungyang, North Korea (Kim et al. 1985). The hominin fossils were assigned to archaic Homo sapiens on the basis of slightly raised brow ridges and a receding forehead. Even though no absolute dates exist for this site the associated fauna suggest deposition occurred during the early part of the Middle Pleistocene (Chang 1989, 1990).

The hominin fossils from Ryonggok cave were originally assigned to Homo erectus on the basis of thermoluminescence (TL) dates of 530-450 ka (Lab of Human Evolution 1995). However, more recent dates, using a combination of uranium series and TL methods, range between 111 ± 10 ka and 44.3 ± 2 ka for cultural layer 2 from which the hominin fossils are associated (Lab of Human Evolution 1995). The hominin fossils were reclassified as Homo sapiens on the basis of these

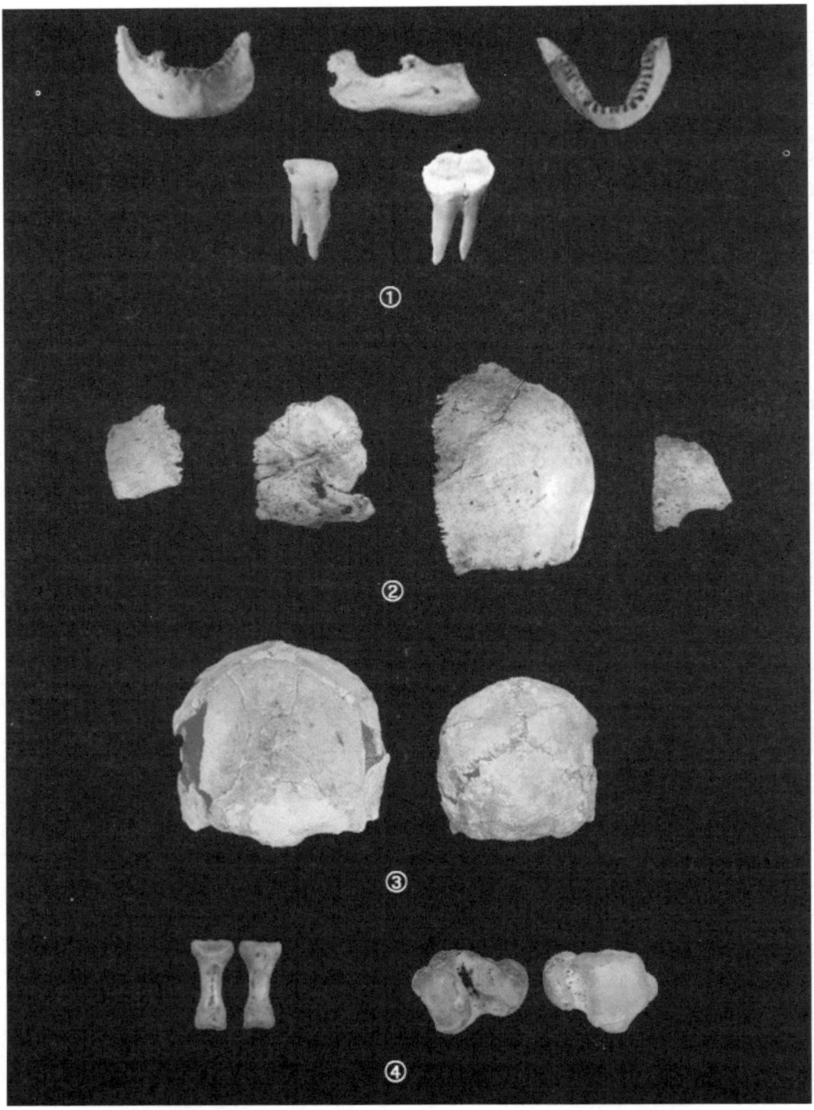

Figure 3-2. Hominin Fossils in Korea

① Dukcheon ② Daehyeondong ③ Mandal ④ Gunang cave

more recent dates and the presence of derived features. Similar hominin fossils were found in Rangjeong cave in Hwanghae Province and are penecontemporaneous with the Ryonggok materials on the basis of faunal correlations (Lab of Human Evolution 1995).

The taxonomic affinity of the earliest hominins in the Korean peninsula is one of the most pressing issues in Korean paleoanthropology. Homo erectus fossils have yet to be clearly reported east of Zhoukoudian in eastern Asia [but the Daehyeondong materials need further investigation (see Norton 2000)]. However, the karstic caves of northwestern Korea may provide the best evidence for Homo erectus fossils on the Korean peninsula, particularly considering the many Homo sapiens localities in the area.

The Earliest Archaeological Sites

Currently, the oldest stone industry on the Korean peninsula is lithic assemblage of the Kommonmoru site. Kommonmoru was discovered in the mid 1960s and was claimed to be the oldest hominin occupation in the country based on the associated faunal assemblage, which is similar to Zhoukoudian Locality 1 (Institute of Archaeology 1969). The faunal assemblage is dominated by extinct species including *Equus sangwonensis K. Gio-gen, Megaloceros sangwonensis Kimsingyu, Macaca sp. Dicerorhinus kirchbergensis Jaeger, Elephantidae gen. sp., Bubalus sp., Cervus nippon grayi.* Other paleoanthropological sites (e.g., Dokchon cave site, Yonggok cave site), on the Korean peninsula have much lower percentages of extinct forms. Currently, no absolute dates exist for this locality. Several specimens present in the cave were identified as sub-tropical species indicating a warmer Middle Pleistocene age (Norton 2000). Only four stone artifacts have been reported, though there may be more (Institute of Archaeology 1977). These include an axe-form, a rectangular shaped piece and two irregular forms. However, these fractured stones representing hominin activity must be questioned because most of the sediments in Kommonmoru represent alluvial deposition; therefore post-depositional processes currently cannot be disproven. Most of these deposits represent gravels and sands formed by the Sangwon river channel, which is presently about 20 m below the cave.

The stone industries from the lower part of Sokchangni have long been claimed to be one of the oldest in the peninsula (Sohn 1972, 1988, 1990, 1993). The site is situated on the lowest terrace of the Keum river in central Korea. A sequence of 27 stratigraphic layers was identified, with the lower part of the stratigraphic column thought to have been deposited during the Early Pleistocene. An AMS date of 50 ka was obtained on a charcoal sample collected from Layer 10 (Sohn 1993). However, the presence of alluvial deposits on the 1st terrace suggests Sokchangni may consist of reworked sediments from an earlier period in the geomorphological history of the river system; thus, the antiquity of the site cannot currently be confirmed.

The stone artifacts from the Keum cave site in the upper Namhan river basin are claimed to be of early Middle Pleistocene age (Sohn 1985, 1990). Paleolithic to Bronze Age cultural materials were recovered in seven stratigraphic layers, with Paleolithic industries (from Lower Paleolithic to Mesolithic) excavated from the bottom 5 layers. The artifacts from the lowest two layers consist of heavy duty tools, such as proto-handaxes and choppers. An electron spin resonance (ESR) date from a rhino tooth from Level 6 suggests a late Middle Pleistocene age (0.18 Ma). However, the excavators assert that this layer should be 0.45-0.35 Ma and the lowest cultural layer to be early Middle Pleistocene (0.7-0.6 Ma; Sohn 1985, 1988). Abundant faunal remains were found in Level 2, including rhinoceros, bear, macaque, and horse. Even though the stone industry and faunal assemblage from the lower layers may be relatively old, it is unlikely that the cave was inhabited before 200,000 BP. The cave is currently just above the modern day river bank. Considering the geological development of the river system in this region, the cave was quite likely inundated for much of the past. Regardless of the age, the archaeological collection is very important because few sites in Korea contain lithics and faunal materials in spatial association. The site formation processes and nature of hominin-carnivore interactions are currently poorly understood at Keum Cave; a situation similar to interpretations of materials from many other cave localities in Korea (Norton 2000).

The Current State of Research on the Oldest Industries in Korea

Due to increasing urban development since the 1970s, more than 150 Paleolithic localities have been discovered in Korea. The vast majority of these sites date to the Late Pleistocene. The few sites that are considered to derive from Middle Pleistocene sediments base these age determination on geo-morphic observations of the surrounding sediments. New applications of various dating methods indicate the potential for developing an in depth chronological sequence from age determinations at these localities.

The Chongokni stone industry, first found in 1978, is often regarded as the oldest lithic technology in the Korean peninsula (Chung 1978; Kim and Chun 1978; Figure 3-3). The stone industry includes many different handaxe forms. The discovery of this site initiated a new discussion on the nature of Movius' hypothesis of a behavioral dichotomy between eastern Asian and European/African stone artifact traditions during the Lower Paleolithic (see Norton et al. 2006 and references therein). In the early stages of research at the Chongokni site, the presence of Acheulean forms was the basis for the assumed Pleistocene age of this locality (Chung and Kim 1979). Based on the morphology of these artifacts the site was suggested to be from somewhere in the Middle Pleistocene. Early attempts to date the locality using radiometric methods have proven difficult. The earliest dating studies suffered from methodological inconsistencies. For instance, age estimations based on the TL method cast doubt on the Middle Pleistocene age of Chongokni (e.g. Yi 1989, 1993). However, contradictory age estimations using the Optically Stimulated Luminescence (OSL) obtained from silt and sandy

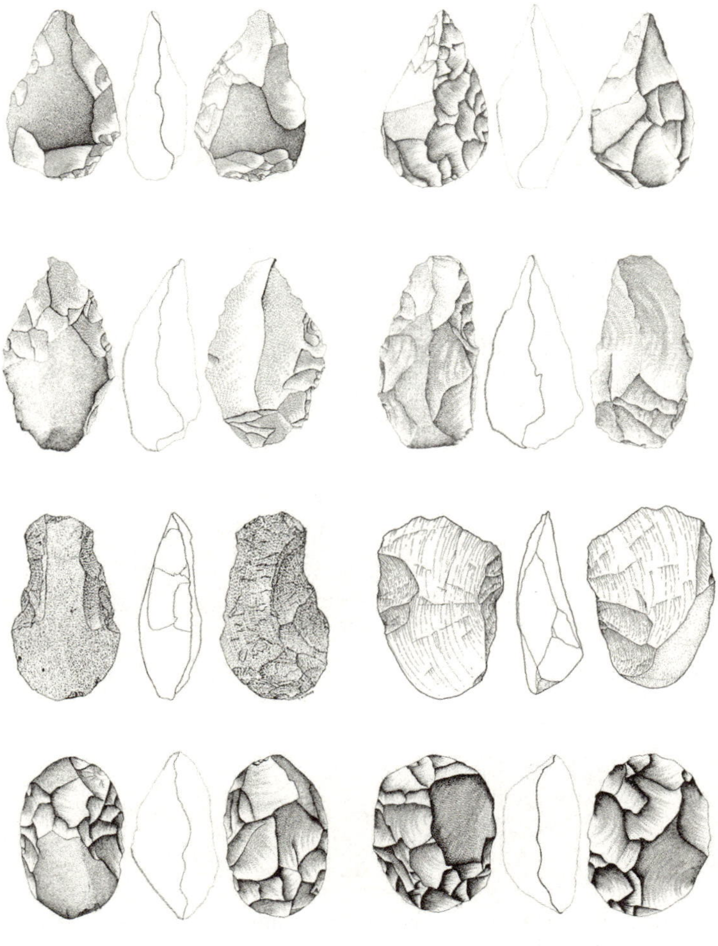

Figure 3-3. Handaxes and cleavers from Chongokni.

deposits at various localities in the HIRB suggested that the earlier attempts to date Chongokni were incorrect (Figure 3-4). Initial attempts to provide a date for this locality resulted in a wide range of ages from earlier than 200 ka to 20 ka

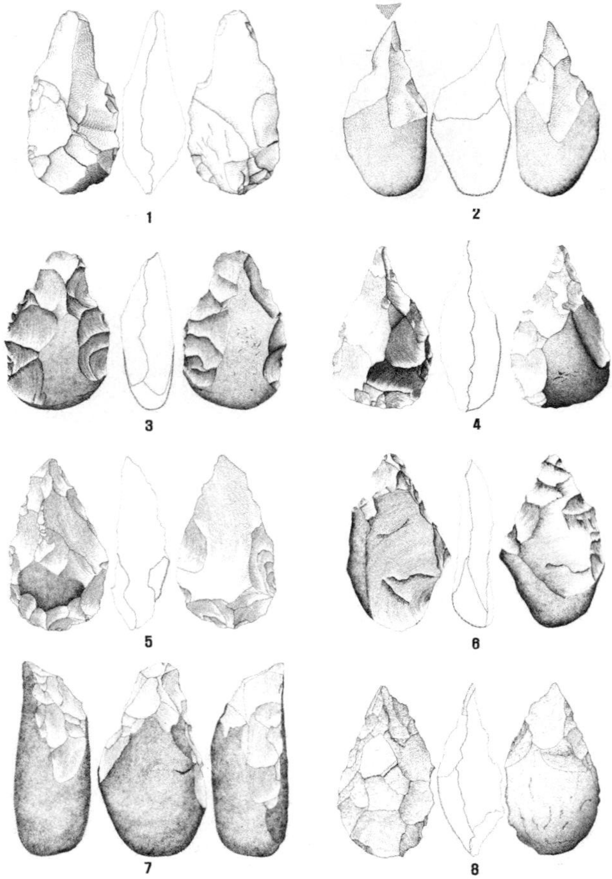

Figure 3-4. Handaxes and picks from various Paleolithic sites in the HIRB
(1. Hoengsani 2.Jangnamgyo 3.Wondang 4.Chuwoli 5.Kawoli 6.Geumpari 7.Jangsani 8.Unjeong).

(Bae 2002, Kim 2010).

Most recently, research carried out by a Korean-Japanese team has determined a new estimation of the age of the Chongokni sediments. The Chongok basalt forming the bedrock of the site was dated to 0.5 Ma using two different dating methods, K/Ar and Fission track dating (Danhara et. al. 2002). Fission track dating was used to date the lacustrine silt that was burned by the emplacement of the underlying basalt. This method indicated a date of 0.49 Ma, while the basalt itself was dated to 0.51 Ma. These dates represent a lower limit for the age of the locality.

Overlying the Chongok basalt are two different types of sediment (Figure 3-5). Lacustrine and fluvial sediments are found directly above the basalt surface. Subsequently a large accumulation of aeolian loess was deposited overlying the lacustrine and fluvial sediments. The lacustrine and fluvial deposits were formed during the time when the ancient river channel was scouring the top of the basalt. However loess deposition, which is believed to be geochemically similar to

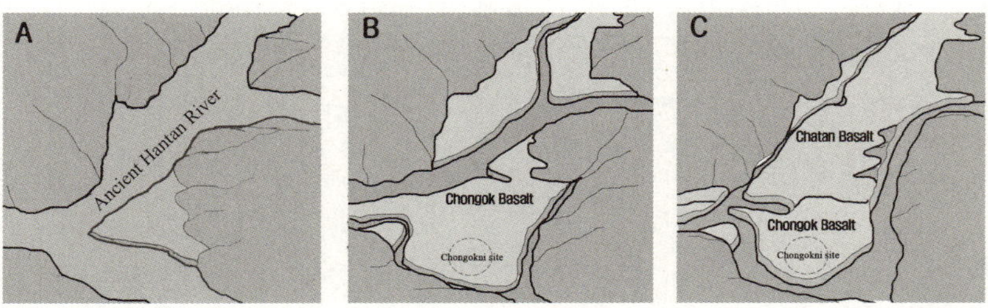

Anceint Hantan River before basalt flow | River channel after Chongok basalt flow (≒ 0.5mya) | Changed channel after Chatan basalt flow (≒ 0.15mya)

Figure 3-5. Developmental processes of the Chongok and Chatan basalts [Modified from Nagaoka (2006)].

Chinese loess (Hayashita 2006), continues into the present. Two different types of tephra originating from pyroclastic eruptions from the Japanese archipelago were identified in the upper part of the aeolian deposit. These two ash lenses were separated by 70 cm and have dates of 25 ka (AT tephra) and 95 ka (K-Tz tephra) (for detailed tephrochronology discussion see Machida 1999). This allows for the construction of a relatively detailed sedimentation rate for the upper part of the loess deposit. The lowermost artifact horizon at Chongokni is found 2.5 meters below the K-Tz tephra, and assuming a constant aeolian deposition rate, the lowest cultural layer should date to 350 ka. One OSL date of 160 ka was obtained below the level of the Kt-z horizon in the same geological trench as the tephra used for K/Ar dating methods (Matsufuji et. al. 2005). Alternating loess-paleosol deposition at Chongokni is believed to represent climatic fluctuations as has been shown in northern China (Naruse et. al. 2003).

The earliest occupation of Chongokni is believed to be older than the advent of loess sedimentation at the site. Stone artifacts were excavated in the fluvial deposits which are overlain by the loess deposit. These artifacts should therefore be considered to be much older than the artifacts found in the loess deposit. Importantly, several handaxes were excavated in situ from a sandy clay layer overlain by this same loess deposit (Kim and Bae, 1983). Based on this new data, the appearance of handaxes predates the 350 ka date for the earliest occupation of Chongokni. It appears likely that the hominin occupation of Chongokni is associated with Acheulean forms well before the Late Pleistocene (Figure 3-6).

In addition to Chongokni several localities in the HIRB are claimed to date from the Middle Pleistocene. For instance, the Jangsanni site near Munsan city in the lower reach of the Imjin river basin is thought to be Early Pleistocene or early Middle Pleistocene (Yi 2002). The stone industry from Jangsanni includes a handaxe found in a colluvium deposit on

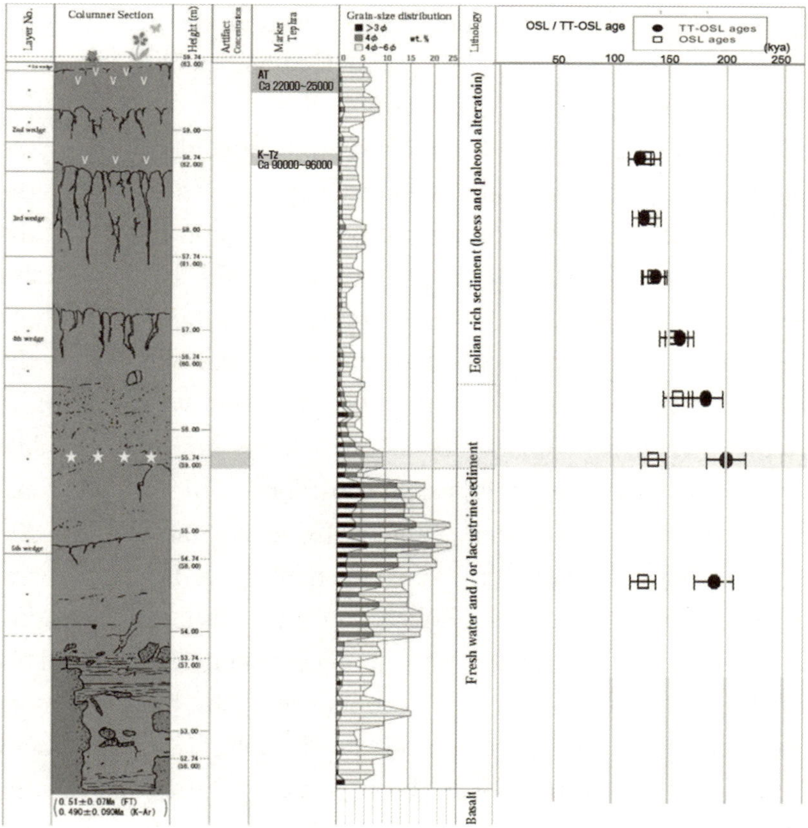

Figure 3-6. Stages of stone artifact variation based on stratigraphic position from Chongokni

the top of a fluvial terrace. This terrace is believed to be the 3rd terrace from the present channel bed, which is situated about 40m higher than the present river channel. Age estimation was based on the geomorphological development of the river terraces in the lower basin of the Imjin River. It is believed that the terrace was formed before the basalt flow in the basin, possibly earlier than 0.5 or 0.6 Ma (Yi 2002). The age of Jangsanni is still under review, and further analyses must be conducted to determine if this locality is contemporary or older than Chongokni.

Aso-4, K-Tz, and AT tephra were recently identified in the upper section of a long depositional sequence from the Mansuri site, west of Cheongju city in the central part of the Korean peninsula (Danhara 2007). Aso-4 and K-Tz tephras are dated to 90 ka and 95 ka respectively. It is not clear how much older the archaeological deposits are that lie below the level of these tephras. It is possible that the lowest level of artefact horizons could be somewhere in the Middle Pleistocene based on stratigraphic position of the two tephras. However, some OSL dates obtained from silty and sandy deposits under the colluvium from which most of artefacts were excavated indicate a Late Pleistocene age, with most ranging between 68 ka and 44 ka, and some between 103 ka and 44 ka. The latter OSL dates were obtained from the fine sediments in the upper part of the stratigraphy (Yi 2007; Park 2010). Another proposal has been suggested that all of the sediment at the site could not be earlier than 75 ka when the 2nd terrace of the Miho river was formed (Kim 2007).

Mansuri is an important locality that warrants further study.

The Jangdongni site in the lower basin of the Yeongsan river in the southwestern part of Korea has also been suggested to be of Middle Pleistocene age. Although archaeological excavation was limited to the upper part of the sequence, extensive geological studies were done on sediments below the excavated horizon (Lee et al. 2003; Lee et al. 2006). The fine sediment of the upper part of the section is believed to be loess/paleosol while the lower part is alluvium. OSL dates on aeolian loess indicate the bottom of the upper strata is older than 220 ka. Therefore, Jangdongni must be from the Middle to Late Pleistocene (Naruse 2006; Lee et. al. 2006). Although no excavation has been carried out in the lowest de-

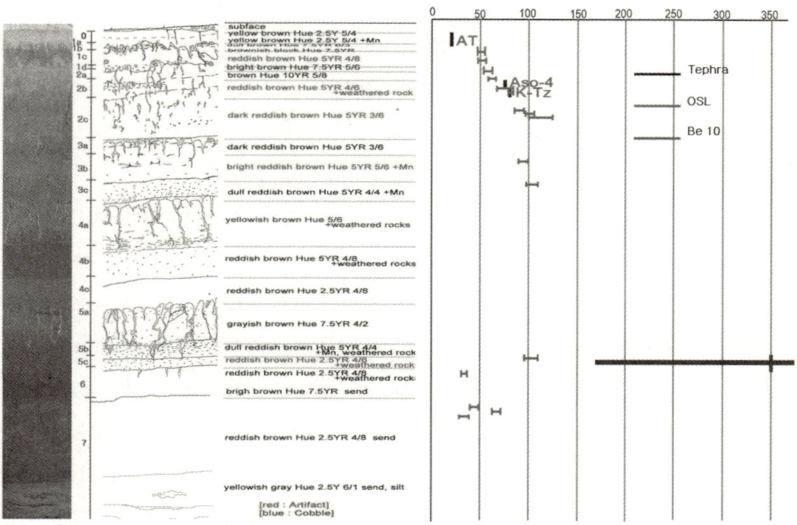

Figure 3-7. Stages of stone artifact variation based on stratigraphic position from Mansuri

posits it should not be surprising if Early Paleolithic artifacts are present at the site.

Although few sites from the Korean peninsula have radiometric dates, current evidence clearly indicates that hominin occupation began sometime during the Middle Pleistocene. Extensive research of the major river basins and limestone caves, especially in the northwestern part of Korea, will surely provide some new evidence for the earliest hominin presence on the Korean peninsula. The unification of the Korean peninsula will be a great catalyst to continuing this research endeavor.

Old Fashioned Artifacts in New Contexts

Developing a chronology of stone industries in Korea is particularly difficult. This is especially true for the assemblages that lack any evidence of a blade or micro-blade technology. Even in those sites that are dominated by laminar industries, crude and expedient tool types appear in association with more developed tool types. This may indicate conservatism in the early stages of stone tool production. However, in some cases, crudely shaped tools may have been derived from earlier pre-existing geological contexts. Other problems include finding a few isolated crude stone artefacts in colluvium deposits on hill slopes are believed to be much older than the age of the sediment surrounding the artifacts. Furthermore, lithics that were surface collected (e.g. Lee 2002) or were found in gravel layers at the bottom of river courses (e.g. Yi and Kong 2004; Jeon and Hyun 2007) are sometimes considered to be remnants of older cultural horizons. Generations of erosional and depositional events have caused the modern day juxtaposition of older artifacts with younger geomorphological features. For instance, at the site of Bongmyoung-dong (Yi and Hong 1999), several Early Paleolithic artifacts may have been eroded and subsequently redeposited in sediments of a younger age. This type of post-depositional history would prove very difficult to determine, even utilizing modern excavation techniques. It is very difficult to determine the amount of time that elapsed between the initial erosion of the artifact and its subsequent deposition in younger deposits. It is generally assumed that Early Paleolithic sites have undergone several episodes of post-depositional modification by erosional processes during the course of the Pleistocene (Bae 2000). This may be the reason for poor preservation of early Paleolithic sites on the Korean peninsula. The exception is the group of localities in the HIRB where volcanic activities modified the channel systems in the basin during the Middle Pleistocene.

What is the Age of the Earliest Occupation and what Types of Stone Industries were Associated with this Earliest Migration?

Multiple lines of evidence presented here indicate a Middle Pleistocene age for the earliest hominin presence on the Korean peninsula. The evidence from Chongokni suggests that hominins appeared possibly as early as 400 ka in the basin. Current geological observations and preliminary analyses, suggest several other localities in the peninsula, including Jangsanni and Jangdongni, could predate Chongokni. In addition, Kommonmoru in Pyoungyang and Keumgul are also considered representative of early evidence of hominins on the peninsula. The Kommonmoru site may be the oldest locality yet known. The fauna associated with this locality suggest the site may be much older than the sites in the HIRB. Yet, there is still some doubt about the nature of the stone artifacts from Kommonmoru. Considering the early age of hominin occupation in northern China there is still the possibility that hominins appeared in the Korean peninsula during the Early Pleistocene. It is quite possible that hominins dispersed along the coastal plain of the current and ancient Yellow Sea into the southern part of the Korean peninsula shortly after their appearance in northeast China. Extensive erosion on the Korean peninsula during the Early Pleistocene would have removed the deposits that would have recorded this initial occupation.

Current evidence indicates that hominins reached the Japanese archipelago much later than the Korean peninsula. After the dust settled from Fujimura's fraud of Early Paleolithic industries in Japan, the Kanedori site in Iwate Prefecture, northern Japan is often considered the oldest site. Stone artefacts from Layer IV of Kanedori possibly date back to the early-middle part of the Late Pleistocene on the basis of tephrachronology (Kikuchi and Yoshiro 2003). The first hominins to have reached the Japanese archipelago is assumed to have migrated from China or Korea during OIS 6 via exposed continental shelves in the Yellow Sea basin and the Korean Strait (Matsufuji 2002).

The discovery of Acheulean-like handaxe forms at the Chongokni site was initially regarded as an exception to the Movius Line (see Norton et al. 2006). However, it would not be surprising if more localities with handaxes are discovered. Localities that have recovered handaxe forms are already known from more than 20 separate places on the Korean peninsula. Early Paleolithic hominins on the Korean peninsula clearly had the ability to produce Acheulean-like bifacial implements. Assemblages that are primarily core and flake tools with a few handaxes and cleavers are referred to as 'Chongoknian' (Bae 1994). Vein quartz and quartzite are the most common raw material for ancient toolmakers during the Pleistocene in Korea. These materials are not suitable for producing typical Acheulean handaxes, because of the numerous joint surfaces in these types of rock. Considering that handaxes have recently been found in China (Hou et al. 2000; Huang 1989; Li 2002), it is quite likely that hominins dispersed into the Korean peninsula with the ability to manufacture bifacial implements sometime during the Middle Pleistocene.

CHAPTER 4

Old artifacts in new contexts: Conservatism? Or Transfomation?

Introduction

Recently, many Paleolithic sites were found in the process of urban development in many areas of the Korean peninsula. Some of the sites yielded old fashioned artefacts, which could be Lower and Middle Paleolithic Age, in disturbed contexts, for example several isolated pieces in colluvium, fluvial contexts or in a context of concentrated on surface of bed rock. It is quite likely to have been transformed by geological processes after original deposition. They consisted of stone artefacts of many heavy duty components shaped crudely. It is very interesting to find some handaxes in the stone industries. These stone industries apparently represent old stage of stone tool development in the Korean peninsula.

Immediately questions to be explained are how they were

formed at the sites?, what is the cultural stage of the industries?, and do the handaxes represent the technological stage of the stone industries? It may not be quite possible to answer these questions, however these questions should be pursued for understanding development of Paleolithic culture in the peninsula.

Sites and Contexts

At some sites in the Han river basin in central Korea, Paleolithic artifacts were found in gravel and snady deposits which were derived from the eroded bedrock. Quartz and quartzite stone artefacts were mixed with angular rocks and sometimes ill sorted coarse sand at the bottom of the sediments. It is believed the layers were apparently disturbed and re-deposited by surface water. In this kind of context, the artefacts are believed much older than the layer from which they came. Concentrations of artefacts occur often at the bottom of ancient ditches or small stream beds. It is observed at some sites in Kimpo and Paju, west of the Seoul metropolitan area, such as Paleolithic sites at Dongbaek (Jeon and Hyun 2005), Shingok, Unjeong etc. In addition to these, similar archaeological contexts were found at some sites in southwestern part of the peninsula. At the Songduri site, the Bongmyoungdong site, even at the Osong site (Bae 2007; Bae Lee and Kim 2006; Kim 2007) near the Chongju, concentration of artefacts of old types were exposed in very coarse sandy colluvium deposits.

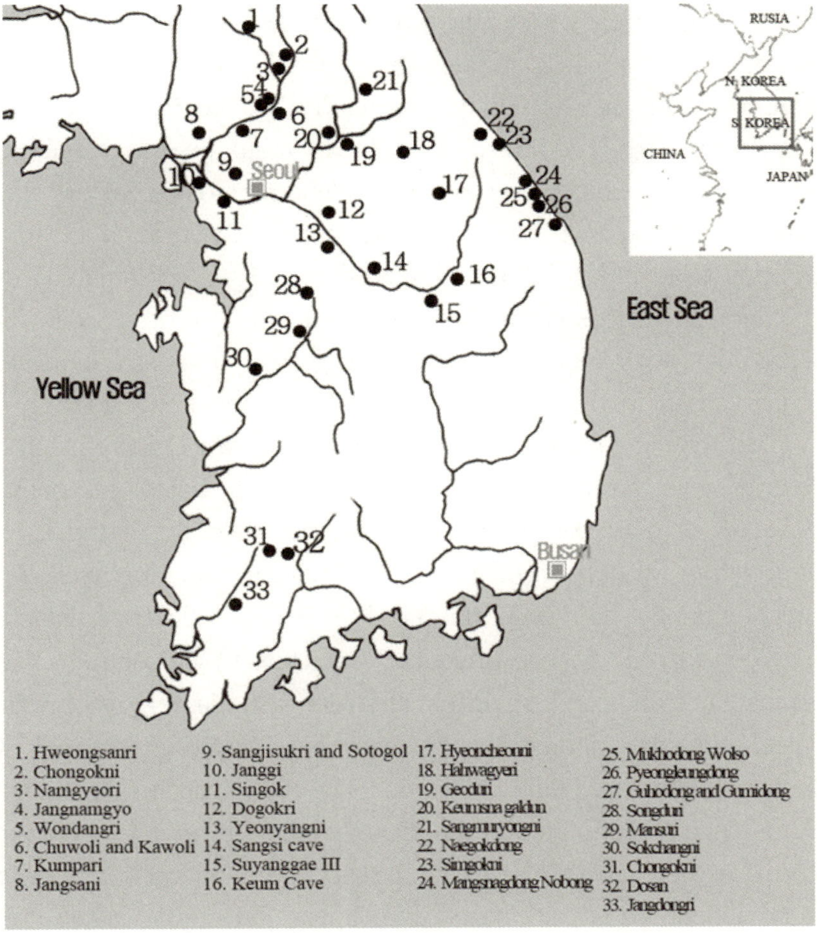

Figure 4-1. Location of Lower Paleolithic site in South Korea

How Old theses Stone Artifacts and what Happened

It may not be easy to make good chronological order for the assemblages that lack any evidence of a blade or micro-blade technology in the Korean peninsula. It has been pointed out that Early and Late Paleolithic Ages would be more appropriate for the chronology of the Paleolithic industries in the Korean peninsula on the basis of current observation of industries (Bae 2001). Even in those sites that are dominated by laminar industries, crude and expedient tool types appear in association with more developed tool types. This may indicate conservatism in the early stages of stone tool production.

The stone industries found below any Upper Paleolithic industries level are considered Lower or Middle Paleolithic ones. However, it may not be easy to tell how old or what the cultural stage would be. This is so, because no clear technological change has been observed in stone industries which are considered to be middle and lower Paleolithic the peninsula. Handaxes are often regarded as one for the lower Paleolithic stone industries, however it is found in stone industries claimed Middle Paleolithic, or even Upper Paleolithic. Chronological definition of handaxe would be another serious topic for the Korean Paleolithic archaeology. At any rate, early stone industries, found below the Upper Paleolithic layer, are not easy to make chronological order on the basis of stone tool morphology and any guess for their ages.

However, in some cases, crudely shaped tools may have

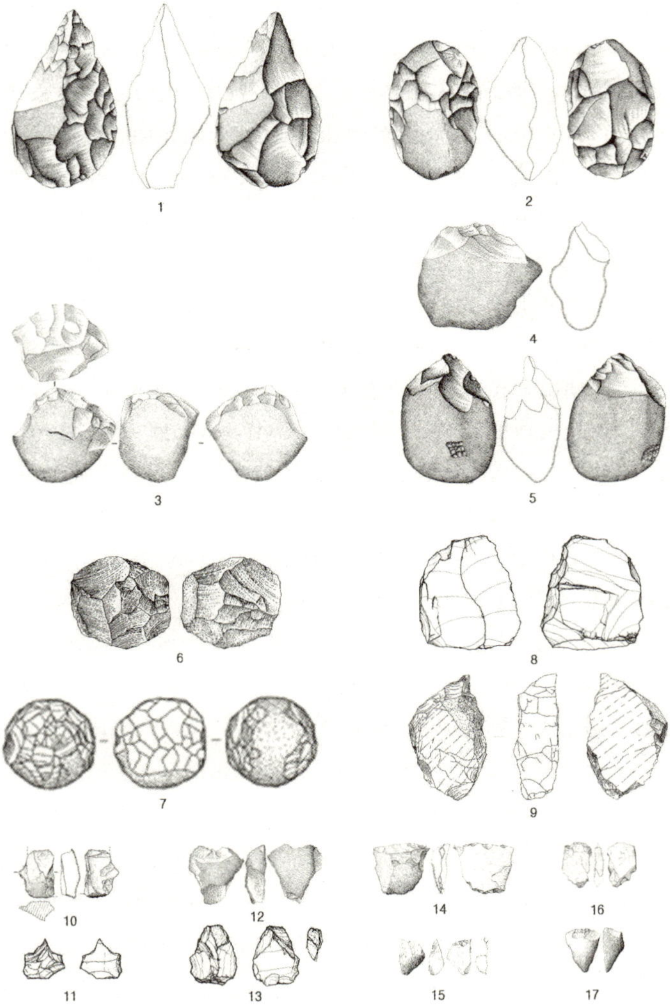

Figure 4-2. Tool types of lower Paleolithic site in South Korea
(1~2 : Handaxe, 3~5 : Chopper and Chopping tool, 6~7 : Polyhedral, 8~9 : H.D.S., 10~11 : Point, 12 : Notch, 13 : Burin, 14~17 : End scraper ; 1,2,4,5,6,8,9,10,11,12,13 : Chonggokni site, 3,16,17 : suyanggae III site, 7 : Pyeongneungdong site, 14,15 : Sangmuryongri site)

been derived from earlier preexisting geological contexts by various post depositional processes. This is especially so because of heavy erosions during the glacial. Other problems include finding a few isolated crude stone artefacts in colluvium deposits on hill slopes are believed to be much older than the age of the sediment surrounding the artifacts. Furthermore, lithics that were surface collected (e.g. Lee 2002) or were found in gravel layers at the bottom of river courses (e.g. Yi and Kong 2004; Jeon and Hyun 2005) are sometimes considered to be remnants of older cultural horizons. Generations of erosional and depositional events have caused the juxtaposition of older artifacts with younger geomorphological features. For instance, at the site of Bongmyoung-dong (Yi and Hong 1999), several Early Paleolithic artifacts may have been eroded and subsequently redeposited in sediments of a younger age. A different case has been observed at the Dangga site in southwestern part of Korea (Lee 2002). This type of post-depositional history would prove very difficult to determine, even utilizing modern excavation techniques. It is very difficult to determine the amount of time that elapsed between the initial erosion of the artifact and its subsequent deposition in younger deposits. It is generally assumed that Early Paleolithic sites have undergone several episodes of post-depositional modification by erosional processes during the course of the Pleistocene (Bae 2000). Similar erosion process is being currently observed in the Isimila site in Tanzania, where channel cut down many different layers from the present surface. Artefacts from layers fall down to the bottom of the valley and mixed. In order to understand the original geological level of the stone artefacts, it is necessary to know geological process of formation of sediment, such as terrace forming, and erosion process in the past. This may be the reason for poor preservation of early Paleolithic sites on the Korean peninsula. The exception is the group of localities in the HIRB where volcanic activities modified the channel systems in the basin during the Middle Pleistocene.

Conclusion

It seems to be true some of old fashioned stone artefacts appeared in industries in late period, Upper Paleolithic industries. Regarding the post depositional process of the Paleolithic sites in the Korean peninsula, some sites have undergone heavy erosion since the primary formation of sites. Some stone industries, even if occurring in geological contexts of later Pleistocene, the age of the stone artefacts would be much older than the sediments which contain them. In the process of disturbance, artefacts of several different ages may have been mixed together into a single layer. This procedure in the sites suggested in the text is believed to have been before the blade technology appeared in most of the sites that have been excavated yet. It is very difficult to know the real age of the stone artefacts assemblages found together in a single layer. As indicated at the Bongmyoung-dong site, whole sequences of original sediments have gone and only remnants of stone artifacts are found on slope of bedrock surface. Considering some stone industries with handaxes turned out to be sometime middle Pleistocene (Norton et al. 2006) and, in particular, the early stone industry with handaxe from the Chongokni site has been date 0.35 mya (Matsufuji et al. 2005; Naruse et al. 2005). The handaxe from the Jangsanni site was claimed much older than this age (Yi 2002). It is generally believed many of these old type stone industries without any blades in Korea could have been derived from sediment of Middle Pleistocene, even early Middle Pleistocene.

Early/Middle Paleolithic Age

CHAPTER 5

Patterns of Early Paleolithic in the Korean Peninsula

Introduction

Hominine dispersal to the Korean peninsula is one of great interested topics in study of human evolution of the World as well as of East Asia because it is situated eastern end of the Eurasian continent. Considering human migration from Africa in human evolutionary history, the peninsula is a destination of human movement. As presence of hominine has been claimed far earlier than 1 million years ago in the mainland China, it has been assumed not quite later than the age of early age of hominines in East Asia. In conjunction with the age of human habitation in the peninsula, it is another interesting topic in Paleo-anthropology of Asia when the Japanese archipelago was occupied particularly, because earlier sites were turned out to be fraud in the mid-1990s. It would be one of most interesting topics in the study of human evolution when hominine could cross large body of water before occupying the Australian continent.

Although rigorous researches have been carried out of Paleolithic industries in the Korean peninsula since early 1960s, several critical questions have been remained to be explained up to now; the lower chronological boundary of introduction of Paleolithic people to the peninsula, unclear typological patterns of early stone industries and conservatism of lithic morphology in the evolution of Paleolithic technology, and the evolutionary relationship between early industries and blade stone industries of the Upper Paleolithic Age. These questions may not be confined not only to the Korean peninsula but to Chinese main continent. Therefore, researches of Chinese Paleolithic industries would be helpful for understanding Korean Paleolithic patterns, however few attempts have been made for explanation of these fundamental questions ever either. Several meaningful discussions were carried out for the reason of this pattern by some western archaeologists (Lycett 2007), but remains still in its early stage of development of relevant explanation.

It is not easy to define 'early' industries in the Korean peninsula, because of very conservative 'tradition' in stone industries in the peninsula and few reliable chronometric dates have been obtained yet. Therefore, chronological system of Paleolithic industries has not been well established at present. Although Lower, Middle and Upper Paleolithic have been often used to describe the chronological order of stone industries, 2 sub-age system of Early and Late, or Lower and Upper, even Middle and Upper, has been proposed (Bae 2002). Particularly, lack of dominant type of technological development, such as levallois technology, before appearance of blade technology is considered to be the most critical for chronology of earlier stone industries. Similar pattern of early Paleolithic industries has been observed in the mainland China.

In this article, review of all current archaeological and Paleoanthropological understandings of available evidences and making a proposition of earliest appearance of hominine in the peninsula are the major objectives. This attempt is expected to provide some relevant insight for more detailed study in future regarding chronology and evolution of Paleolithic industries.

Hominine Dispersal into the Korean Peninsula

It is one of the critical issues in Paleolithic archaeology in Asia when the first hominine arrived far eastern end of Eurasian continent before they got the Japanese archipelago possibly in sometime of the Upper Pleistocene. Considering the early age of hominine occupation in northern China, there is still the possibility that hominine appeared in the Korean peninsula during the Lower Pleistocene although no proper evidence is available at present. It is quite possible that hominine dispersed along the coastal plain of the current and ancient Yellow Sea into the southern part of the Korean peninsula shortly after their appearance in northeast China, because no geographic barrier had been in routes of dispersal and favorable environment throughout the Pleistocene.

However, very few hominine fossils were found up to now and are mostly turned out Homo sapiens. Hominine fossils were found in limestone caves sites in North Korea except one example found in the Shangsi cave, Tanyang, South Korea. Fragments of human bones from caves site in the central part of South Korea were claimed, but too fragmentary to identify specific hominine type. Among those found in North Korea, Deokchon man, Yeokpo man and Yonggok man were assigned to rather old type of Homo sapiens, while rest of fossil men, Mandal man and Seungnisan man were classified modern Homo sapiens. As none of these fossil men can go back before 200,000 BP, it is quite unlikely they represent earliest appearance of hominine in the peninsula considering that the Jinniushan Man in the Liaoning province has been dated 270,000 BP. The Jinniushan man is the oldest fossil man in the east of the Zhoukoudian cave site and suggests expansion of hominine into the peninsula occurred at least in this time range along the coastal region of the peninsula even if continental shelves was not exposed. Human fossil evidences found in the Korean peninsula up to present may not be considered representing any early forms of hominine of the early stage of dispersal into the peninsula.

Chronology Framework of Stone Industry

Chronology of early Paleolithic has not been well established in the Korean peninsula due to few reliable dates of stone industries. Since the first radiocarbon method was applied to the charcoal from the Seokchangni Paleolithic site and obtained 32,000 BP in early 1970 (Yang 1972), various methods have been applied. However, due to lack of datable materials in archaeological deposits, few reliable dates were obtained and results from other methods than Radio carbon method or AMS had been disputable and controversial. Estimation of age of industry is often attempted on the basis of geomorphological context of sediments, for example position of river terraces on which Paleolithic artefacts were found. Regrettably, even vertical desiccation cracks in sediment have been considered as an indicator of certain time period of the Pleistocene, but it is unlikely because such natural phenomenon can be observed any time of similar environmental condition.

Recently increasing number of OSL dates were obtained from many sites particularly in the central part of the Korean peninsula. OSL dating method is very useful for dating sediments in which no other datable material has been found. Most of dates obtained turned out not older than 100,000 BP except those from those aeolian sediments, loess, of the Chongokni site. The middle level of the sediment was dated older than 160,000 BP and 200,000 BP by OSL and TT-OSL (Kim 2009). In spite of frequent use of OSL dates in Korean Paleolithic archaeology, couple of problems remain to be explained in future researches. Some of OSL dates are not match well with outcomes of AMS. In addition, OSL dates from the Mansuri site show some abnormal order because ages of upper level were turned out older than those from lower level. Although current OSL dates are referred as tentative evidence for understanding age of the sediment or industries found in it, we may need to be patient to get more reliable dates of OSL and of other methods of dating in future.

Due to lack of any distinguishable development of debitage technology, it is very difficult to make any chronological order of stone industries before appearance of blade technology in the Upper Paleolithic. Most of the industries in this period consist of handaxe, choppers, polyhedral, various types of cores, some small shaped tools including becs and denticulates, etc. They are shaped with minimal retouches for making edges, therefore often called 'expedient' or casual. Three Age System, Lower, Middle and Upper, is commonly used for describing chronological position of particular industry, however no distinction in typological and technological traits can be made for the industries considered belong to Lower and Middle. It has been suggested to use two sub-stage system, Lower and Upper, or Early and Late for Paleolithic industries of the Korean peninsula. Similar pattern is found in the Paleolithic industries in the Chinese mainland. However, it is still being under discussion for making relevant chronology for explaining evolution of industries. Tentatively in this article, stone industries before the presence of blade technology are classified as 'Early' Paleolithic for discussion of pattern.

Contexts of Early Paleolithic Industries

Early Paleolithic sites were found in various geological contexts including fluvial terraces, colluviums, loess deposits, ancient channel beds etc. Early industries were often found lower layers below Upper Paleolithic layers in river terrace deposits and many of them are often described as 'Middle' Paleolithic. Similar strategraphic contexts are found in colluviums developed on hill slope. In fact, few Paleolithic artefacts were found in fluvial deposits of river terraces, while many were reported from colluviums or aeolian deposits on the top of terraces. At the 3rd locality of the Suyanggae site, artefacts were found on gravel deposit which is a fluvial terrace. They were possibly derived from deposits higher than level of presence. At the Bongmyoungdong site in Cheongju city, many large pieces were exposed on a natural trench on a relatively abrupt slope, however no Quaternary sediment was observed on the top of the hill at all. In this case, it is not possible to estimate the rough age of the sediment even though the upper boundary of age could be suggested from age estimation of currently observed sediments. From observation of various geological contexts in which stone artefacts were found, some of stone artefacts found in colluviums deposits could have been derived from very old sediment that eroded away long time ago.

Stone artefacts fund at the bottom of ancient stream channels or trenches formed on bedrocks may have been formed in a same kind of depositional processes as the one at the Bongmyoung-dong site. Artefacts which had been deposited in earlier but vanished sediments slowly and gradually moved to lower and bottom of valleys as sediments had been winnowed or eroded away slowly at sites. All original sedimentological contexts had been gone and some of stone and natural cobbles remain at lower area. In these cases, it is almost impossible to figure out how old artefacts or industries are, because age of sediment is often quite younger than the age of stone artefacts. Winnowed remains of stone artefacts have been found at many localities in the Korean peninsula: Songduri in Jincheon, Dangga in Naju, some localities of Mansuri site in Cheongwon, Janggi and Shingok in Kimpo, many localitites in Unjeong, Paju, etc. Huge mixture of Paleolithic artefacts and cobbles of angular forms and rounded were exposed at the bottom of sediments of sites in Kimpo and Paju in the lower Han river basin. It is quite likely that flow of water on land surface and fluvial channel activities at bottom of small valley during the warm periods after cold and dry climate would have been reasonable explanation for sedimentation processes of this kind. It is interesting to note many of these sites are situated in western part of the peninsula where west wind usually brings lots of moisture from the Yellow Sea. Chronometric dates, OSL and AMS dates mostly, of sediments above these winnowed sediments were often turned out older than 40,000 BP. It is very likely that these ages represent the upper boundary of the stone artefacts at the bottom. Even so, it cannot represent age of original geological contexts if no other means of dating methods or estimation is possible.

Early stone artefacts were found in huge thick fine sediments, some of which have been claimed loess deposits. Particularly, loess deposits are observed at many localities in the HIRB. Although there are some disputes on the origin of the sediments, claims of colluviums or Aeolian from exposed continental shelves during glacial period, particularly during the LGM, some fine sediment found in the inner area of the peninsula, eastern mountain range, is also claimed loess deposit which were blown from Inner Mongolia or northern China during the Pleistocene. Long-distant transported quartz grain was reported from some localities (e.g. Pyoungchangni) and similar depositional structures are observed many Paleolithic localities in the Jiangjang river basin and sites in Shandung province in China. Although loess deposits in the Korean peninsula are relatively thinner than those in China, properties and structure are similar

Several localities were intensively investigated by scientists and archaeologists. Among them, $E_{55}S_{20}$ pit of the Chongokni site, Locality 1 and 4 of the Mansuri site and the Jangdongri site in Naju were analyzed with various scientific methods including age dates. In these localities, many alternative horizontal bands of loess deposit and soil formation were observed in vertical section of sediments, which is considered to represent climatic cycles during sedimentation. Vertical cracks in sections indicate ancient surface or eroded surface at level of the upper most part of the cracks, which are often mentioned as 'patterned ground' by frost action or wet-dry episodes. At the

Chongokni site and the Mansuri site, two types of volcanic tephras were identified with some interval in depth; AT near the surface and K-Tz about 70 ㎝ below the AT horizon. These two tephras, which provide valuable clue to understand rate of aeolian sedimentation at the site, are usually considered age of 25,000 BP and 95,000 BP in Japan. Recently, a new dating method, $^{26}Al-^{10}Be$ method, was applied to the Chongokni and the Mansuri sites. Rocks from layers of artifact concentration or piece of artefacts were directly dated by this method and turned out very old ages, from 400,000 BP to 700,000 BP. Difference of age dates from different methods should be discussed for explanation of depositional processes and may need some more dates for reliable range of age of these sites.

The stratigraphy of the Jangdongni site, Naju, southwestern part of the Korean peninsula shows a long sequence of deposit of fine clayish sediment on relatively coarse sandy deposit. It is not know yet how deep the sediment goes to underground. OSL dates of the fine sediment turned out from 200,000 BP to 20,000 BP while age of the lower part of the deposit is not known although magnetic reversal was observed between fine and coarse sediment. It may be the first occasion in Pleistocene deposits ever investigated in the peninsula. Stone artefacts were found only from the upper layers which were dated mostly Upper Pleistocene. Because very small area was excavated up to now, it remains uncertain how much deep artefacts will be found at this site. The fine sediment of this site is considered aeolian, while lower coarse sediment is possibly fluvial or overback floodplain deposit by the ancient Yeongsan river system. It is not clearly known where the source was of the fine sediment.

Patterns of Stone Industries

Stone industries before the appearance of blade technology in the Korean peninsula are mostly crude and primitive shape due to lack of elaborate retouches and advanced technology of debitage in preparation of cores and flakes, although crude look may be derived from crude raw material, quartz vein and quartzite in almost of all industries. Tool types mostly consist of bifaces and unifaces, choppers, polyhedral, core scrapers, scrapers, becs, points, denticulates, notches, ect., as shaped tools, and cores and flakes in addition small pieces of waste. Shaped tools were made with minimal secondary modifications and accordingly look crude and 'expedient', casual works for immediately use of tools at needed places. It is very likely that most of choppers, cores, heavy duty scrapers and polyhedral were used for detaching flakes as well as tools for specific function. Even, bifaces and unifaces were possibly modified continuously for flakes before disposal at sites. Among the shaped tools, in addition to biface, polyhededral is common as a pattern of compositions.

It is notable that bifaces among heavy duty components are the most extensively fabricated tool type. Couple of handaxes are present in many of early Paleolithic sites, while some sites such as the Chongokni and Jangnamgyo sites yielded many pieces of various types. Some patterns are observed in debitage process to get final forms. Cobbles, particularly flat ones preferred, big flakes detached from large river cobble and irregular shaped chunks were used for blanks. Relatively large portion of primary form often remains on final products because relatively few pieces were extensively retouched. Large portion of butts remains minimally modified for handling and reducing total size and accordingly often thick. It is often observed that pieces were shaped with minimum number of flaking for desired edge or form. Even so, there are some tendencies in form in terms of length, weight and rate of symmetry.

Among handaxes, pointed types are more common including pick-like and pick. There are some variations on their edges, real pointed one and chisel ends, horizontal or inclined. However few pieces have long cutting edges on sides, which indicate these types are not a kind of large cutting tool, as in Acheulean proper. Ovate types are often shaped on flat cobble by flaking unifacially on both sides in opposite directions and section of body normally is shaped trapezoidal. Context surface usually remains parallel on opposite sides. Although some of this type were extensively retouched, it is notable that no sharp cutting edge is observed. Cleavers are mostly atypical with few flaking on both sides except some typical ones and many big modified flakes are often used as cleavers for cutting.

Polyhedral are one of the most characteristic and most common heavy duty tool types in early stone industries. There are some variations in forms, degree and way of debitage process and size; drum type, peach type, globe type etc. These variations can be explained as a different stage of reduction of cores. However, is should not be neglected that they were a multiple purposed tool type, core and tool with specific function, as in some cases of handaxes. Spheroids and even stone ball - like ones are occasionally observed, but in most cases irregular globular shapes. Abundance of these tool types along with cores of various stages may indicate that flake was commonly utilized for various purposes, cutting and scraping without extensive modification.

Small tool types include scrapers, notches, becs, denticulates, points, etc. Few were made by extensive retouches on various kinds of primary forms. Even in some cases, it is not certain what intended function was. Therefore, it is not easy to build up typology for these tool types, due to limited number of these types appeared in a single industry. It is very hard to observe a pattern in small tools. As stated above, flakes may have been used quite often as small tools for various purposes.

Conclusion

Early Paleolithic industries before appearance of blade technology are often mentioned as expedient type, because unclear intention of edge modification with limited secondary retouches. Heavy duty components such as handaxes and cleavers, polyhedral and choppers are representing characteristic feature of early Paleolithic industries, while some types of small tools also appeared. Handaxe is present from the earliest stage of 'early' Paleolithic at some sites such as the Chongokni site. Various types of handaxes are present in most of the 'early' Paleolithic sites. Along with handaxes, presence of different types of polyhedral is also one of the patterns in this age. Both heavy duty components might have been used for multi-purposes, core for flakes and tool for specific heavy duty. From this aspect, flakes without secondary modification could have been used for various occasions.

Questions, such as 'how old?' and 'what type of hominines were responsible for these tools?', cannot be answered clearly because few relevant evidence are available at present. However, stone industries from the Chongokni and Mansuri sites could be Middle Pleistocene of their ages. In particular, earliest stone industry from the Chongokni site, Stage I of the Chongokni industries, is very likely older than 0.35 mya on the basis of various chronometric dates of the sediments. Stone industries from layers below the cultural layers 3 of the Mansuri site could be as old as those from the Chongokni site if Al^{26}–Be^{10} dates are considered reliable. In addition to these two sites, there are some stone industries in the HIRB and the lower Han river basin could be as old as these. It is very reasonable to consider that 'early' Paleolithic industries, expedient type with handaxes, are as old as middle Middle Pleistocene although it is not certain yet when the first hominine dispersed into the Korean peninsula after arrival in northeastern China in earlier time than 1 mya.

CHAPTER 6

History of Handaxe Studies in Korea

Introduction

Since the first find at the Chongokni site in 1978 in the Korean peninsula brought an extensive discussion against validity of Movius' hypothesis. The new evidence has been found not only in Korean peninsula but in China. Current archaeological data suggest obviously presence of handaxe in East Asia. However, no agreements has been made on morphological classification and nomenclature due to lack of sophisticated forms and low frequency in an industry. Several critical issue of Acheulean-typed in East Asia include origin of handaxe, chronological change of technology and terminology of handaxe industries. The major object of this paper is to review current studies of handaxe in Korea and to propose new direction of researches in the future to make some explanation of issues above.

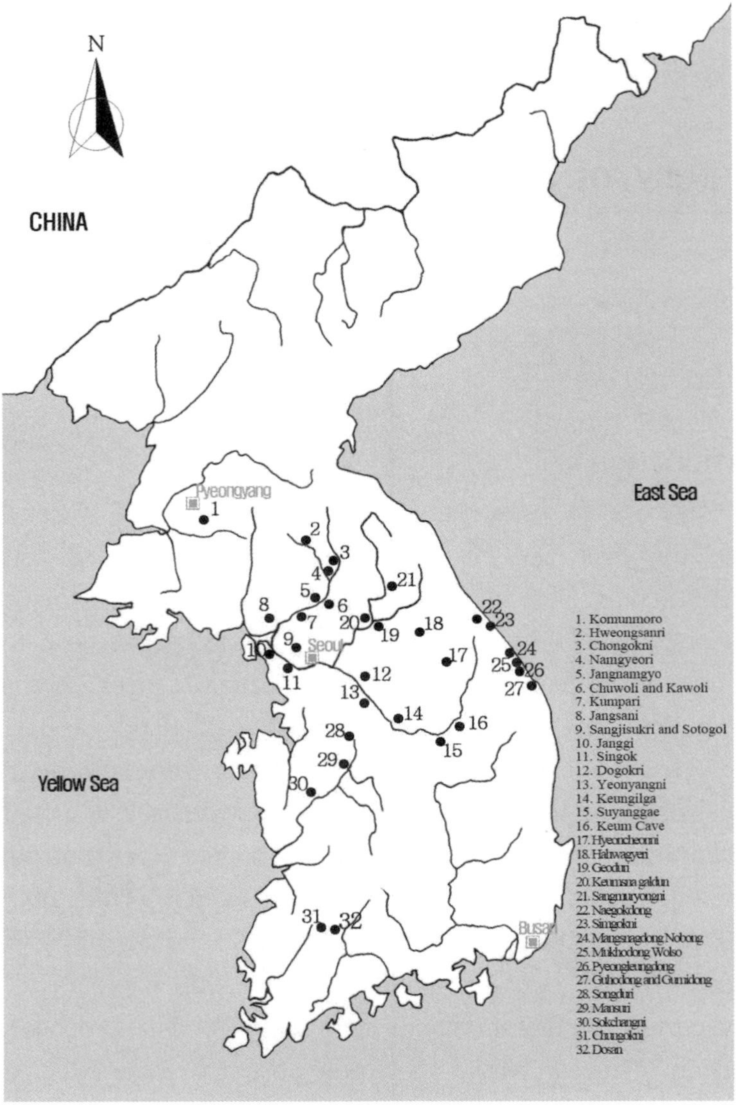

Figure 6-1. Handaxe sites in Korea

Distribution and Context of Handaxe sites in Korea

Most of handaxes were reported form sites in the central part of the Korean peninsula although some were found in south-western part of the peninsula (Figure 6-1). In particular, sites are concentrated in the Han river basin and the HIRB. Handaxes from sites in southwestern park of the peninsula are considered relatively late, presumably Upper Paleolithic Age on the basis of presence of developed type of tools. Most of sites in the lower reach of the Han river basin, in Kimpo and Paju, were transformed heavily through several re-depositional processes from original dispositions. In these sites, handaxes were found in deposits of angular cobbles mixed with coarse sandy sediment. Similar archaeological contexts were observed at some sites in the mid-west region, such as Songduri and Mansuri sites. While, many of handaxes in the Hantan river basin were found in layers of fine sediment, possibly, loess deposits although some were clearly found in sandy layers at the lower part of deposit.

Morphological and technological variations

Handaxes from the Chongokni site were classified into many different types devised by F. Bordes (Chung 1978); ficron, lanceolate, amigdaloid, ovate etc. The most frequent type is pointed one crudely shaped leaving thick butt, some of which often called pick-like, or trihedral form in previous Chinese terminology. Another typical type is ovate shape. It should be particularly notable that some of this type were very extensively retouched but thick body. Some forms of cleaver on flake also appeared in the industries in the HIRB.

Most of handaxe components were made on quartz and quartzite cobbles, while some on big flakes. Cleavers are mostly made on big side-blowed flakes, however few are typical ones with modification on both sides. As most of heavy duty components do not have any sharp side edges for cutting, in may not be proper to classify these components as Large Cutting Tools as in Africa. Edges are mostly formed on tip for pointed or chisel end. Few pieces were shaped with extensive retouches while many were shaped by limited number of flaking in spite of obvious planning for tool making. In most cases, surface of primary form remain on final shape. In general, these heavy duty components do not show strict regularity in flaking process and shaping. This is so because of nature of raw material, quartz-vein or quartzite material which is the most common raw material in Korea. These raw materials are very hard to take off flake and have often internal joint surface along which rocks are tend to be broken accidently in the course of tool making.

Four types of technique of making handaxe are observed (Bae 1983). Types are distinguished by primary forms for tools. The first one is technique of shaping bifacial handaxe on big flake. In most cases, they are relatively thin and retain some cutting edge. The second is ovate handaxe on cobble.

Some of this type were shaped very extensively on peripheral edges, however still very thick body without any cutting edge on sides. In this type, some forms of trapezoid can be included in this type because they are shaped on same kind of primary form, in most cases broken piece of flat cobbles. The third type is unifacial handaxe on big flake or broken piece of cobble. In this case, heavy duty pointed tip is made on distal end of thick primary form. The fourth type is pointed handaxe, or rather may be called pick with a heavy duty point shaped on tip with unretouched body and butt. In addition to these, some big flakes with minor modification can be classified into handaxe. Except ovate handaxe type, few pieces were extensively retouched although they are clearly considered a certain type of handaxe. Most of cases were formed by minimum retouches leaving large flake scars and wide cortex cover on their surface.

Age dating and chronology

Another issue is how old they are? There was a controversy of earliest age of handaxe from the Chongokni site which is possibly the oldest. An age of 0.3–0.4 mya was suggested on the basis of morphological comparison of handaxes with European Acheulean at the time of find(Chung 1978).

Early TL dates did not support the age, but were considered an age of about 40,000~50,000 BP of the handaxe industry from the Chongokni site (Yi 1983). As lack of proper material to date with relative accuracy, age determination of handaxe industry in the Korean peninsula remained one of hot topic in Paleolithic archaeology in Korea.

Scientific analysis at the Chongokni site indicates that sediment on the top of basalt at the Chongokni site had been formed from the middle part of Middle Pleistocene to late Upper Pleistocene by aeolian process, so called loess. This estimation of age of 0.35 MYA for the lowest horizon of stone artefacts of $E_{55}S_{20}$ pit is based on aeolian chronology, OSL dates, tephra chronology, K/Ar dates and fission track dates. ^{26}Al–^{10}Be dates obtained from the lower horizon of the Jangnamgyo site was turned out 0.25 MYA, where many different types of handaxes were found. In general, it is believed that handaxe industry in the Korean peninsula probably appeared earlier than the mid Middle Pleistocene. However, recent AMS dates obtained from charred wood below basalt in the vicity of the Chongokni site suggest much younger than previously existing dates, younger than 40,000 BP (Yi 2009). It suggests much extensive work should be done to date handaxes in Korea.

Acheulean? or Chongoknian in Asia

Many handaxes have been reported in China since the first one at the Chongokni site in Korea. The most important one is the handaxes from the Bose site in southern China. It was dated back to early part of Middle Pleistocene. Recently, many

Acheulean-like handaxes were found at the Luonan Basin in central China. Although accurate age is not known, it is believed to be some time in early Middle Pleistocene on the geological observation of loess sediment (Wang 2008). In addition, many localities are known now in the central China along the Jianjang river basin. In addition, it should be noted that there are many forms that can be classified into handaxe among some of stone industries which were called 'Large Trihedral Industry' such as industries from Dingcun, Kehe and Gonwangling site etc.

It is obvious that handaxes are present in East Asia from these finds. However, there are conflicting views whether these finds could be considered 'Acheulean' or some other local name of industry, such as 'Chongoknian' suggested in early studies (Chung 1978; Bae 1992).

During the last 30 years after the first appearance Acheulean-typed handaxes at the Chongokni site, Movius hypothesis has been criticized and revised based on new typological views. In spite of all, handaxes from Korea and China are generally not very much different from those classified as Acheulean in Europe and Africa in terms of technological evolution. However, we still have to point out there are some differences. Few typical types with thin section and long cutting edges with extensive retouches are not present in East Asia. In addition, it needs to be mentioned that no site has ever been found with high concentration of handaxes as the Isimila site or Ologeseilie in East Africa. It seems that handaxe technology in East Asia did not develop up to a level of

Acheulean of Europe and Africa in terms of at least frequency and refinement. At present, there are different views regarding this pattern of handaxe industry of the World. Raw material, vein quartz and quartzite, may not be proper to reach to finest level of tool forms, while another possible explanation is different adaptive process. Recently, 'Bottle neck phenomena', limits of raw material, morphological diversity from adaptive process, etc. are suggested for the explanation of these phenomena (Northon et al. 2009).

Conclusion

During the last 30 years, it has been a hot issue in Paleolithic archaeology of world to explain patterns of handaxe in the World. In recent years, more and more diverse and reasonable hypothesis have been proposed to explain distribution pattern and morphological variations. However, it is still not well enough to eliminate all questions raised up to now. Another important thing to consider is increase of new evidence in East Asia. A new synthesis with comparative studies of handaxes in the World may bring a new insight of cultural evolutionary processes in different part of World during the Pleistocene. Particularly in Korea, various types of handaxe appeared in sites in the Han river basin and the HIRB would be a potential evidence to answer some questions regarding technological process of tool making and function of tools considering relatively well established chronology of excavated materials.

CHAPTER 7

The Movius Line sensu lato (Norton et al., 2006) further assessed and defined

Introduction

Previously, we outlined a model of the Movius Line sensu lato(s.l.) to describe the relative paucity of bifacial implements in Pleistocene East Asia (Norton et al., 2006). We made three general observations (Norton et al., 2006: 534):

"· Compared to East Africa and India, the frequency of handaxe sites in East Asia is significantly lower.

· The percentage of bifaces in these East Asian lithic assemblages is usually much lower than coeval sites from India and East Africa.

· East Asian handaxes are not morphologically similar to typical western Old World Acheulean implements (based on thickness here, but also in other attributes and dimensions)."

Petraglia and Shipton (2008) agree with our first two observations, but in light of their re-evaluation of the biface data from the Luonan and Bose basins in China and the HIRB in Korea, they argue for a significant amount of overlap between metric data from bifaces east and west of the Movius Line. In so doing, they reject our third point that the bifaces from these two regions are morphologically different. Even though this third observation was only a minor point in the Norton et al. (2006) defined Movius Line s.l. model, we welcome the opportunity to more fully investigate questions about East Asian handaxe morphology, in addition to clarifying a few points in our earlier paper. There are three primary areas that we discuss: 1) morphology of the East Asian handaxes; 2) sample size and distribution; and 3) age of the HIRB sites and Luonan Basin sites. Statistical analysis was done in SPSS 11.5.

Morphology of the East Asian handaxes

Petraglia and Shipton (2008) use biface metric data to support their argument for morphological similarities between bifaces east and west of the Movius Line. For instance, they note that when measuring handaxe thickness, the material from Olduvai Bed II (East Africa) and Mudnur VIII (India) are greater than or within the range of the Korean and Chinese localities. This leads them to conclude that "while the Acheulean localities tend to have thinner implements in general, thickness does not, in itself, discriminate handaxe morphology across the Movius Line" (Petraglia and Shipton, 2008: 963). The mean values as presented by Petraglia and Shipton (2008, their Table 1) do show that the average thickness of the Olduvai Bed II and Mudnur VIII implements is greater than or within the range of that of the East Asian materials. However, the 18 other lithic assemblages in their table all have means much lower than the Korean and Chinese materials. A Mann-Whitney U-test comparing their western Acheulean thickness data against their East Asian thickness data is statistically significant (Mann-Whitney U= 7.0; Exact p=0.007). Not only is there a significant difference in mean thickness, but it might be argued that the Olduvai Bed II and Mudnur VIII bifaces cannot be used in comparisons with the East Asian materials, particularly because: 1) temporally the Olduvai Bed II handaxes are early Pleistocene, whereas all of the East Asian materials are middle and/or late Pleistocene; and 2) the Mudnur VIII bifaces are considered unfinished, while there is no reason to believe the East Asian handaxes are also unfinished. Petraglia and Shipton (2008) note both of the above reasons as explanations for the thickness of these particular assemblages.

Nevertheless, in these types of analyses we suggest that simple presentation of descriptive statistics is of limited interpretative value. In light of the limitations of using univariate measures to examine variation in handaxe morphologies east and west of the Movius Line, we propose that the recent application of multivariate morphometric methodologies (e.g., Lycett, 2007a, b; Lycett and von ramon-Taubadel 2008) be used to address these questions in the future. For instance, instead of relying solely on unilinear variables (e.g. width, length, thickness), Lycett (2007b) measured 60 different quantitative metrics on core nuclei. In short, methods such as Lycett's multivariate research approach are significantly more robust and convincing than the univariate data analyses presented by Petraglia and Shipton (2008) and, we admit, than those in our own original paper (Norton et al. 2006).

Sample size and distribution

Petraglia and Shipton (2008: 962) note that in their study, "When available, our analysis attempts to examine the range of variation between localities, rather than by coarser level comparisons between basins." This is an important distinction that we feel is necessary to discuss, particularly because how a data set is aggregated or divided has important implications for the ensuing analysis and resulting interpretations. Petraglia and Shipton (2008) use the data from the Luonan Basin, China as the basis for their argument to discount the Movius Line s. l. as defined by Norton et al. (2006), so we begin there.

As of 2007, there are 236 handaxes and 119 cleavers reported from the Luonan Basin fieldwork (Wang 2005, 2007). In Petraglia and Shipton's (2008) comparative analysis they group all of the handaxes and cleavers from all of the Luonan Basin sites together, although doing so conflicts with their argument that it is better to make site-by-site comparisons rather than basin-by-basin comparisons. However, they do not present the precise number of sites in the Luonan Basin from which these bifacial implements are derived; in fact, these lithics were collected from 268 open air sites and lithic scatters (Wang 2005, 2007; Wang et al. 2007), a value much higher than the> 60 sites mentioned at the base of Petraglia and Shipton's (2008) Table 1. A second, but equally important point that is not mentioned is that handaxes and cleavers (n = 355) represent just 2.6% of all artifacts found in the basin (n = 13,581; Wang et al. 2007). Finally, a third important point that is not discussed is the large size of the Luonan Basin. The basin is 70 ㎞ east to west and 20–30 ㎞ north to south (~ 2,100 ㎢; Wang 2005). This translates to finding an average of 0.88 handaxes per site, or 1.32 handaxes/cleavers per site, or 3.37 handaxes per km walked east to west. Even in the HIRB, where the numbers are substantially lower than what is found at many sites in India and East Africa[as noted by Petraglia and Shipton (2008), often hundreds of sites with hundreds of bifaces (e.g., Olorgesailie, Kalambo Falls)], handaxes are still found in greater frequency than in the Luonan Basin (HIRB: 4 sites, 58 handaxes = 14.5 per site).

Even if one accepts the Luonan Basin handaxes as typical Acheulean we suggest that finding, on average, < 1 handaxe per site over such a large area does not warrant arguing that a "true" Acheulean tradition exists in East Asia. Instead, Luonan Basin stone toolkits are dominated by core and flake tools (> 97% of artifacts), a pattern similar to the HIRB collections and one which is referred to as "Chongoknian" (Bae, 1994).

Age of the HIRB sites and Luonan Basin sites

Based on Yoo's (2007) doctoral dissertation, Petraglia and Shipton (2008) suggest that the HIRB materials are younger in age than we suggested, although they never state how old. In fact, Yoo (2007) argues that the lithic toolkit from the most representative HIRB site (e.g. Chongokni) is middle late Pleistocene (~60 – 45 ka), whereas we suggested the oldest cultural deposits date to 350 – 300 ka (Norton et al. 2006). Our age calculation was based on bracketing dates of 0.5 Ma and 0.095 Ma on underlying basalts and overlying tephra, respectively, and a steady rate of deposition. Indeed, the hominin occupation may be even older since handaxes have been excavated in situ from the sandy clay layer that underlies the thicker loess layer (Kim and Bae, 1983; Bae in press).

We emphasize a point here that we did not make fully in our earlier papers concerning the HIRB materials (e.g. Norton 2000; Norton et al. 2006) and which is important to contextualizing the age of these materials. It should be remembered that the Korean Peninsula was never completely separated from the Chinese mainland during the Pleistocene, and during periods of lower paleobathymetry Shandong Province (eastern China) was connected to the Korean

Peninsula (see Norton 2007 for paleobathymetric reconstructions during the late Pleistocene-Holocene in the region). If Homo erectus populations appear at nearby Zhoukoudian (Shen et al. 2001) and Huludong (Wu et al. 2002) between 800 – 400 ka it is quite plausible for hominins to have reached the Korean Peninsula during that time interval, or shortly thereafter. In fact, evidence for this may be present in North Korea at the site of Komunmoru, which is broadly comparable to Zhoukoudian Locality 1 on biostratigraphic grounds (Norton 2000).

Although it is beyond the scope of this paper to more fully discuss the question of the age of the Korean handaxes, there is growing evidence that the earliest peopling of the Korean Peninsula likely occurred sometime during the middle Pleistocene. Even the foremost proponent of the "young" age for the Chongokni handaxes (e.g., Yi 1986) has excavated sites (e.g., Jangsanni) and materials in the HIRB that are probably of middle Pleistocene age (Yi 2002). New studies at sites like Mansuri and Keum Cave also suggest the strong possibility that hominins reached the Korean Peninsula by at least the middle of the middle Pleistocene (see Bae in press).

While at least some of the HIRB specimens we analyzed are from stratified and dated contexts, the handaxes from the Luonan Basin analyzed by Petraglia and Shipton (2008) were all surface collected or derive from unclear contexts (Wang, 2005). Even though Petraglia and Shipton (2008) acknowledge the uncertainty of the ages, they include these materials in their analysis, which we consider unwise. Although recent studies have suggested a middle Pleistocene age range (780 – 144 ka; Lu et al. 2007), the Huaishuping and Mayigou sites were recently dated by optically stimulated luminescence to between 90 – 50 ka (Wang et al. 2007). Since all of the bifacial implements come from unclear contexts, it might be possible for them to be terminal Pleistocene or even early Holocene in age. We think this latter scenario to be unlikely; however, until the sites and materials from the Luonan Basin are better studied and described, the interpretative value of finding <1 handaxe per site remains to be established.

Defining the Movius Line sensu lato (Norton et al., 2006)

Norton et al. (2006) defined the Movius Line s.l. by making three salient observations about: a) the number of sites in East Asia that have handaxes, b) the number of handaxes at each site, and c) the morphological variation between the handaxes east and west of the Movius Line. We did not argue that typical Acheulean handaxes are never present in East Asia, although one could read Petraglia and Shipton (2008) to imply that we did. It is a well-known fact that in certain cases the East Asian handaxes are similar in some respects to those found west of the Movius Line, particularly the African Sangoan (e.g. Clark 1982, 1994; Yi 1986, 1989; Bae 1988, 1994, 2000, 2002; Schick 1994; Norton 2000). Thus, this observation is neither surprising nor new.

In addition to the points we note above, there is growing evidence of handaxes in regions where they were previously unknown. For instance, handaxes and associated tektites were recently excavated from in situ deposits of the Damei and Fengshudao sites in the Bose Basin (Wang et al. 2006). Handaxes have also been identified in the Danjang Reservoir localities in Hubei Province (Li 2007). Like a few of the bi-faces from the HIRB and Luonan Basin, some of the handaxes from Damei, Fengshudao, and Danjang resemble typical Acheulean bifaces. However, as with previous findings of heavy duty tools at basins/localities like Bose, Luonan, Dingcun, and the HIRB, the bifacial components of the re-spective lithic collections are proportionately very small, and for the most part, look different than a typical Acheulean.

As we have noted previously (Norton et al. 2006: 534), even "'if a map of East Asian Paleolithic sites were drawn, the conspicuous lack of biface-bearing sites in East Asia is still prominent, despite over 80 years of paleoanthropological re-search in this region of the Old World." Only when Paleolithic archaeologists working in East Asia begin to find hundreds of sites with bifaces, and each of these sites have hundreds of typical Acheulean bifaces, will we feel a strong argument can be made to fully reject or reconfigure the Movius Line s. l. (Norton et al. 2006). Finding one, or even a few, "typical" Acheulean handaxes at a site east of the Movius Line is not grounds for dismissing the boundary. A quarter century ago Yi and Clark (1983) used this same argument and failed to convince the greater scientific community. We contend that the case is not substantially different today.

There are a growing number of inter-regional comparative studies of Paleolithic bifacial technologies between Africa, India, and East Asia (e.g. Leng and Shannon 2000; Noll and Petraglia 2003; Norton et al. 2006; Lycett 2007a; Lycett and von Cramon-Taubadel 2008). Even though future studies may prove otherwise, current published archaeological data still strongly supports all aspects of the Movius Line sensu lato as defined by Norton et al. (2006). This includes the additional data presented by Petraglia and Shipton (2008).

CHAPTER 8

Middle Pleistocene handaxes from the Korean Peninsula

Introduction

The ability to produce bifacially worked stone tools is often viewed by paleoanthropologists as a major cognitive breakthrough. Once it became evident that handaxes, cleavers, and picks (i.e. Acheulean tool complex or Mode II technology) postdated the earliest core and flake industries (i.e. Oldowan tool complex or Mode I technology), paleoanthropologists associated the production of these more refined heavy-duty tools with more advanced hominin behavioral and cultural patterning such as enhanced planning aptitude, learning ability, technical competence, long range mobility strategies, and possibly symbolic thought. This correlation is based on the justifiable assertion that Mode II stone tools display a degree of standardization not evident in Mode I technology (Gowlett 1986). We now know that the Acheulean stone toolkit initially appeared in Africa by about 1.5 Ma (Asfaw et al. 1992) and spread to other regions of the Old World, although the Oldowan core and flake tool complex continued to appear into historic times (Kleindienst 1961; Roe 1964, 1968, 1981, 1994; Leakey 1971; Isaac 1977, 1984; Toth and Schick 1986; Potts 1988; Wynn and Tierson 1990; Schick and Toth 1993, 2001; Gowlett and Crompton 1994; Wynn 1995; Foley and Lahr 1997; Klein 1999; McPherron 2000; Villa 2001; Noll and Petraglia 2003).

One of the most interesting questions in Paleolithic studies is related to the regional variation in the presence/absence of the more technologically advanced Mode II tool complex of the Pleistocene Old World, particularly East Asia. The root of the query is that in many regions of the western Old World, handaxe-bearing assemblages appear to have phased out the original Oldwan core and flake toolkits, whereas in the eastern Old World there appears to have been continuous production and utilization of Mode I implements. This dichotomy is known as the "Movius Line," after the Harvard archaeologist Hallam Movius who first noted the distinction between Acheulean industries in the western Old World and the apparent absence of refined bifaces east of the Indian subcontinent (Movius Line sensu stricto; Movius 1944, 1948, 1969). Since Movius' observations, there has been ongoing dialogue in the paleoanthropological literature regarding this behavioral dichotomy (e.g. Luchterhand 1978; Aigner 1981; Yi and Clark 1983; Pope 1989; Schick and Dong 1993; Clark 1994; Pope and Keates

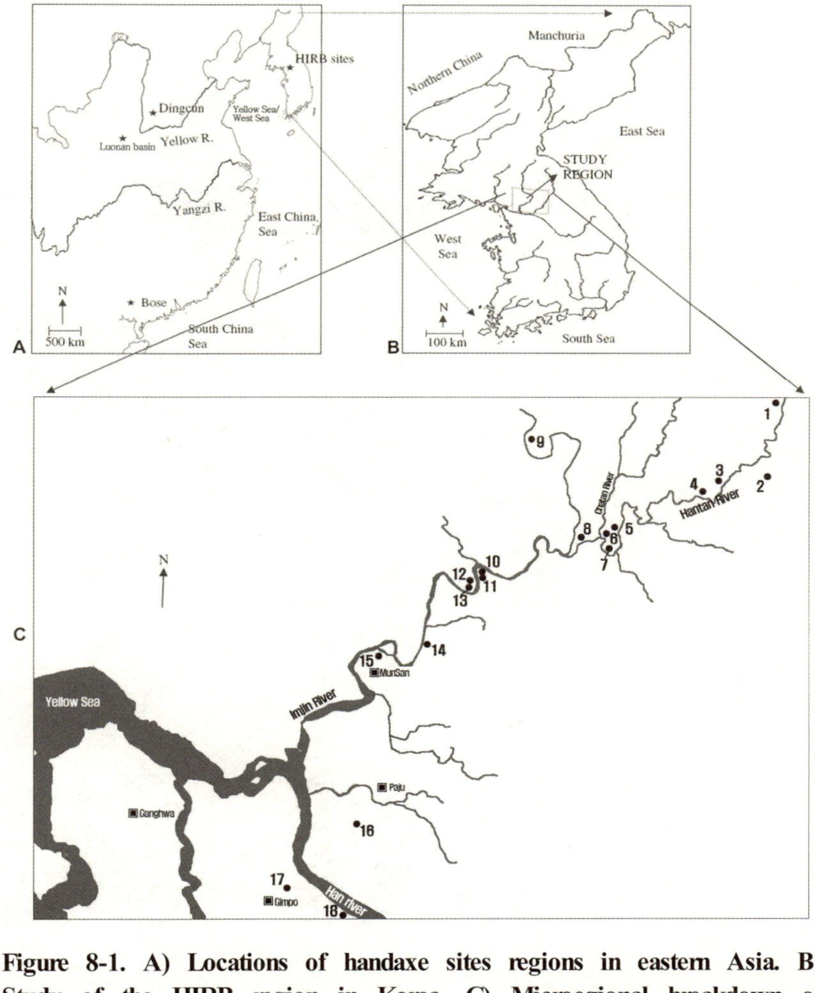

Figure 8-1. A) Locations of handaxe sites regions in eastern Asia. B) Study of the HIRB region in Korea. C) Microegional breakdown of HIRB

(1. Jangheungri 2.Uncheon 3.JungriNeulrori 4. Chongokni 5.Namgyeori 6.Heongsani 7.Gawoli 8.Chuwoli 9.Wondangri Jangnamgyo 10. Wondangri 11.Keumpari 12.Jangsani 13.Unjeong 14.Janggidong 15.Shingok)

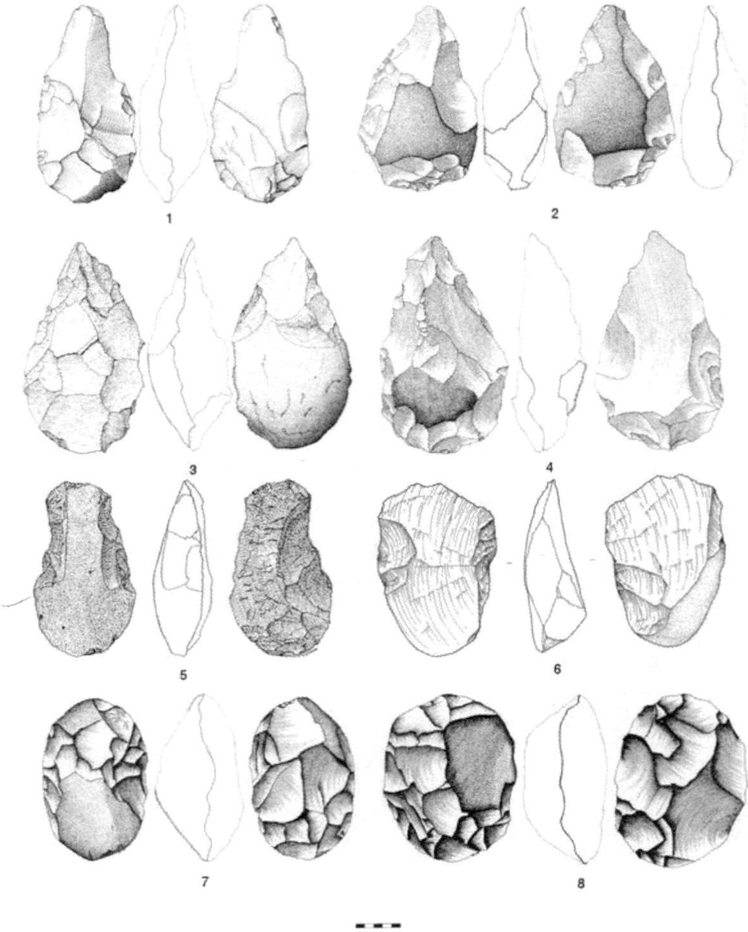

Figure 8-2. Handaxes of Paleolithic sites in Hantan-Imjin river basin.

1994; Schick 1994; Larick and Ciochon 1996; Petraglia 1998; Leng and Shannon 2000; Hou et al. 2000; Keates 2000, 2002; Corvinus 2004).

We present a series of biface assemblages from Middle Pleistocene deposits of the Korean Peninsula and compare these with those from India and Africa. The handaxes that form the foundation of this study were discovered over the past quarter century from a series of open-air Early Paleolithic localities in the HIRB in Korea (Chongokni, Kumpari, Chuwoli, and Kawoli). Furthermore, two localities in China (Dingcun, Bose) are considered in which handaxe-like implements have been discovered both in situ and as surface finds. The HIRB handaxe assemblages are then compared to the better-known biface collections from Olorgesailie (Kenya) and Hunsgi-Baichbal (India) to explore inter-regional variation east and west of the Movius Line. In this paper, we utilize the two stage cultural model ("Early" and "Late" Paleolithic) proposed by Gao and Norton (2002) because the three stage Paleolithic sequence ("Lower," "Middle," "Upper") normally applied in Old World prehistoric research is not applicable in East Asia, particularly China and Korea.

Hantan-Imjin River Basins (HIRB) sites

Early Paleolithic handaxes were discovered in the HIRB region in the spring of 1978 just outside the town of Chongokni (see Figures 8-1 and 8-2). Chongokni is situated on a basalt plateau with mountains to the east and low hills and flat plains to the west. The present day Hantan River flows between the basalt plateau and the low-lying mountains, although it is assumed that the path of the river fluctuated throughout much of the Pleistocene. Surveys and excavations were conducted at Chongokni beginning in March 1979 under the direction of Professor Wonyong Kim, then Director of the Seoul National University Museum, and researchers from other archaeological institutes. Since the initial discovery of hominin occupation at Chongokni, the area has been surface surveyed and excavated 11 times, resulting in the discovery of over 5,000 heavy-duty tools, flake implements, and debitage. In particular, the 1994-1995 field excavation revealed a high concentration of in situ artifacts and debitage (Figure 8-3; Yi 1989; Norton 2000; Bae 2002).

As a result of surveys and test excavations in other zones of the HIRB, a number of additional Paleolithic sites have been discovered (see Figure 8-1). The best known and published of these are Kumpari, Kawoli, and Chuwoli. Two separate localities were discovered just outside the village of Kumpari in 1989 during archaeological surveying by the Department of Archaeology, National Research Institute of Cultural Properties (NRICP). Kumpari is located along the lower end of the Imjin River, only a short drive from Chongokni. Between 1989 and 1992, four excavations were carried out by the NRICP under the direction of Kidong Bae. As a result of the fieldwork, almost 3,000 artifacts produced primarily of quartz and quartzite were recovered from two

Figure 8-3. Artifact horizon (level E94N65-I) from the 1994-1995 Chongokni field season.

Figure 8-4. Example of oval depression from Kumpari (in closest test pit). Note the higher density of lithics in the depression as opposed to the outer area.

localities. Ten oval depressions with heavy concentrations of artifacts were discovered at Kumpari (Figure 8-2). The depressions are irregularly shaped, and it is not clear how they were formed. However, it has been suggested that these sites may represent areas utilized for repeated stoneknapping (Bae 1992, 1998, 2002; Bae et al. 1999).

Paleolithic artifacts were discovered in Chuwoli and Kawoli in the spring of 1988. Additional surface survey and small-scale excavation of the two localities in 1993 led to the discovery of some 600 lithic artifacts, many produced on quartz and quartzite, with a smaller percentage on olivine basalt. Most of the stone tools were flakes and debitage, while a few handaxes and cleavers were also discovered during the fieldwork (Yi and Lee 1993; Yi 1996). In 2005, approximately 200 more lithics were discovered during renewed excavation work at Kawoli by Hanyang University.

Except for the low percentage (5%) of handaxes, picks, and cleavers in the HIRB lithic assemblages, there are no distinctive differences between the Korean Early Paleolithic collections and many of the coeval northern Chinese collections (e.g., Zhoukoudian Locality 1) that are represented primarily by cores, small flake tools, and debitage (Figures. 4-7). Hominins manufactured the HIRB stone tools by direct hard-hammer percussion. The majority of the heavyduty and flake tools lack secondary modification (e.g., retouching), and are considered expedient and casual in nature. The primary raw materials utilized at the HIRB sites are local vein quartz and quartzite river cobbles. Unlike many of the Middle Late

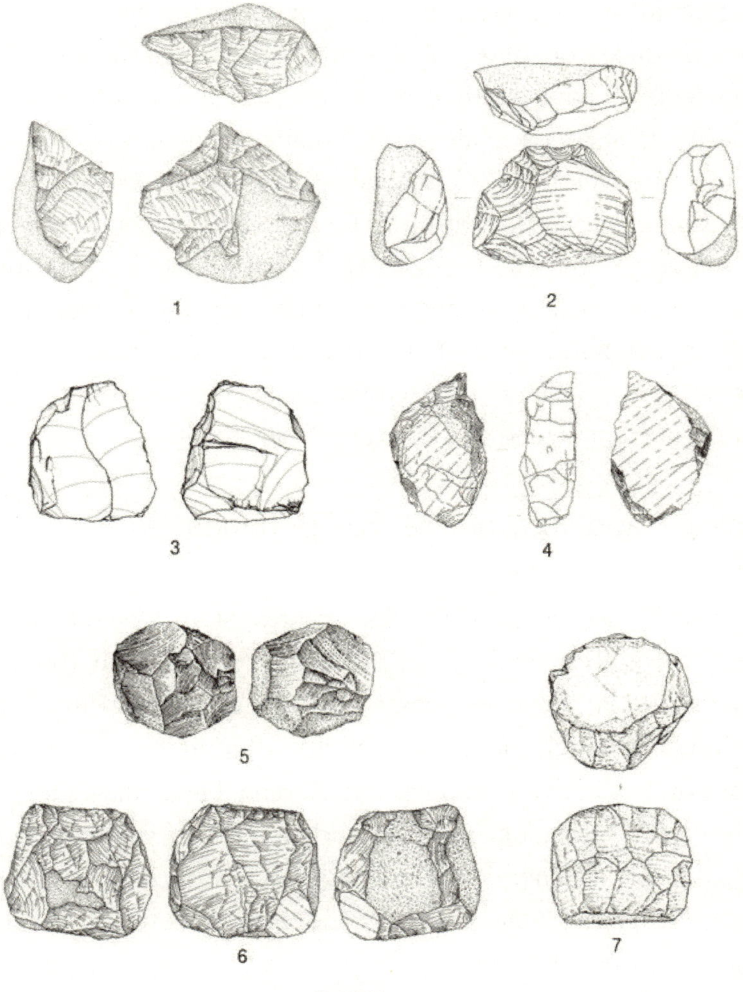

Figure 8-5. Stone tools of Chungokni site
(1, 2 : chopper 3, 4: H.D.S. 5~7:polyhedral)

Pleistocene Chinese lithic assemblages, the HIRB toolkits do not contain stone spheroids, although many polyhedrals exist. Being produced on river cobbles and thick in nature, the HIRB stone toolkits have often been noted for their resemblance to the African Sangoan, albeit not quite as advanced in their manufacture (Yi 1989; Yi and Lee 1993; Clark 1994; Bae et al. 1995; Bae et al. 1999; Norton 2000; Bae 2000, 2002). Bae (1994) has suggested that East Asian Early Paleolithic accumulations that have a small percentage of bifaces should be referred to as "Chongoknian". Overall, these assemblages should still be considered a variation of Mode I technology since the stone toolkits are dominated by core and flake tools.

Geology and age of the HIRB handaxes

The HIRB are located in the southwestern region of the Chugaryeong Rift Valley, which runs from Seoul in the west to Wonsan on the east coast. The Chugaryeong Rift Valley developed through tectonic activity during three primary stages and effectively divides the Korean Peninsula. The first stage of rift formation occurred during the Precambrian and is composed of Yonchon and Gyeonggi gneiss. This phase represents the base of the Chugaryeong Rift Valley. The second stage developed during the Jurassic and Cretaceous and is represented by the Tongjai and Jantanni Basalt strata. The most recent phase is the crystallization of the Baekyuri gravel layer and the Chongok Basalt level, both thought to have formed during the Pleistocene (Figure 8-6). On the basis of field observation and chemical analysis, at least two basalt flows (and possibly as many as six) have been identified within the Chongok Basalt layer in the IHRB with chronometric dates indicating a Middle Pleistocene age (ca. 0.5 Ma: derived through K/Ar and fissiontrack methods). More detailed

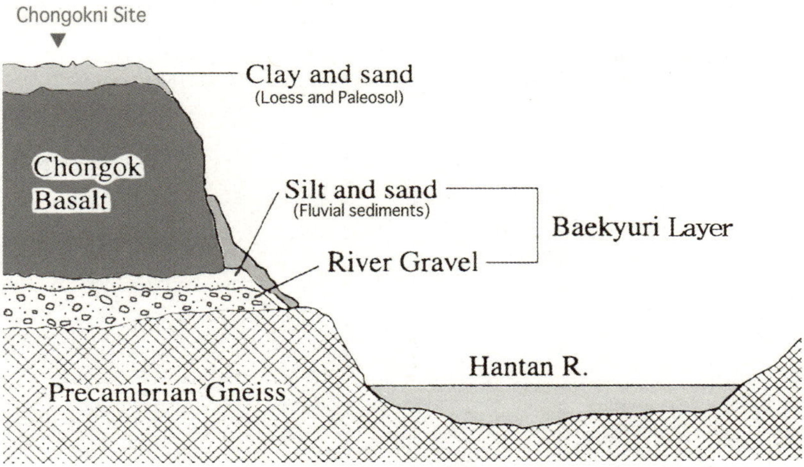

Figure 8-6. Geological section of the IHRB near Chongokni

geological studies of the basalt are difficult because the majority of the IHRB is situated in the currently inaccessible demilitarized zone separating North and South Korea. The Chongok Basalt stratum, where the Early Paleolithic stone toolkits have been discovered, forms a horizontal basalt plateau that covers the Baekyuri gravel layer. The sediment that overlies the Chongok Basalt has been eroded by natural geological processes as well as by recent cultural disturbance, which have facilitated the discovery of Pleistocene materials through surface surveys and excavation (Bae 1989; Yi 1989, 1996; Bae et al. 1999; Danhara et al. 2002).

Since the initial discovery of the HIRB assemblages, chronometric dates derived from the various layers of the Chongok Basalt have resulted in a wide range of dates (Yi 1996; Bae 1997, 2002, 2003; Yi et al. 1998). A recent analysis focused on the longest stratigraphic profile of the sediment on the basalt

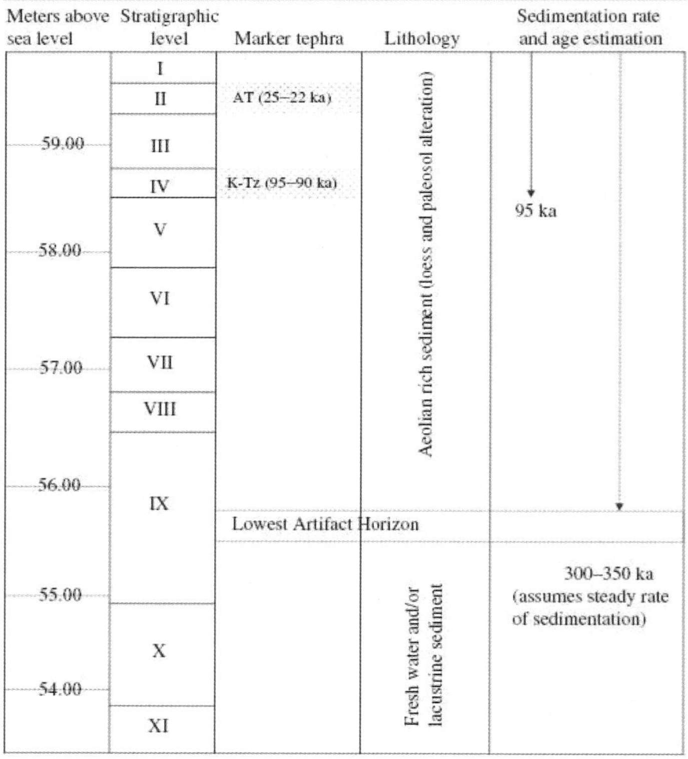

Fig. 8-9. Stratigraphic profile of Chongokni site correlated with tephra markers, lithology, and reconstructed sedimentation and age estimations (after Danhara et al. 2002)

bedrock that is situated in the southern area of the Chongokni site ($E_{55}S_{20}$). This profile can be divided into 11 separate stratigraphic layers (level I: top layer, most recent; level XI: base of Chongok Basalt, oldest), with artifacts found as low as level IX (Figure 8-9). AT (Aira-Tanzawa) tephra (25-22 ka) was discovered in level II, and K-Tz (Kikai-Tozurahara) tephra (95-90 ka) was identified in level IV. These tephras originated from a volcano in Kyushu, Japan, and their appearance in Korea and the Shandong Peninsula in northern China are the result of two major volcanic eruptions that occurred during the Late Pleistocene (Machida 1999). Utilizing fission track and potassium-argon dating methods, Danhara et al. (2002) determined that the base of the Chongok Basalt has an age of 500 ka. The lowest levels are thought to be the result of stream channel or lacustrine sedimentation, and Danhara postulated that those levels (X-XI) had a higher rate of sedimentation (see Fig. 8-9). However, since some of the artifacts, including handaxes, from Chongokni are derived from level IX, assuming a steady sedimentation rate for levels I-IX, it has been estimated that the lowest artifact-bearing level should date to between 350-300 ka (Danhara et al. 2002). Even though Danhara''s analysis concentrated on determining the age of the lowest artifact-bearing level of the excavation pit from Chongokni, due to similarities in depositional histories, it appears that a chronometric age range for the other HIRB sites comparable to that at Chongokni is very plausible (see Yi 1989, 1996; Bae 1989, 1997, 2002, 2003; Yi et al. 1998; Danhara et al. 2002 for detailed discussion involving the chronometric age of Chongokni and other localities in the HIRB).

Bifaces east and west of the Movius Line

Over the course of the past half-century, several East Asian paleoanthropological localities have been discovered that do not conform to the patterns associated with the "Movius Line." These sites have exposed evidence of technologically advanced heavy-duty stone implements (i.e. handaxes, picks, and cleavers) east of the line. The three best known localities are the Chinese sites of Dingcun in the north (Movius 1956; Pei et al. 1958; Qiu 1985), Bose in the south (Huang 1987, 1989; Hou et al. 2000), and as discussed above, the Korean sites located along the HIRB.

Dingcun was the first of these biface-bearing sites identified east of the Movius Line. Located in Shanxi Province in northern China, Dingcun was discovered in the spring of 1953 by local workers digging for sand along the Fen River. Dingcun is a series of sites (14 to date) found scattered along a 15 km stretch of the Fen River where archaic Homo sapiens fossils, other Pleistocene animal remains, and stone tools have been discovered both as in situ finds and as surface collections.

Due to similar depositional histories, the Dingcun localities are often discussed as one site. Based on an array of uranium-series, electron-spin-resonance dating, lithostratigraphic, and biostratigraphic studies, the age range of the Dingcun localities is between 210-75 ka, although most of the chronometric dates appear to fall around the Middle-Late Pleistocene transitional period. Since Dingcun is actually a series of localities and not a single site complex, it is difficult to obtain a narrower chronometric age range. During the initial excavations, three deciduous hominin teeth and a partial subadult parietal bone were discovered at Locality 54:100; these remains represent at least one archaic Homo sapiens individual (Movius 1956; Pei et al. 1958; Qiu 1985; Wu and Poirier 1995).

The Dingcun lithic assemblage comprises over 2,000 implements, including large flake tools and stone spheroids (also known as "bola balls"). These artifacts are produced from high quality hornfels that is exposed naturally in rocky outcrops roughly 10 ㎞ west of Dingcun (Pei et al. 1958; Qiu 1985; Gao 2000). Direct percussion and bipolar techniques were utilized in the manufacture of these assemblages.

Some evidence of platform preparation is present as well. Dingcun is best known for the presence of picks and cleavers, some of which measure upwards of 18 cm in length. This differs from the more traditional East Asian lithic assemblages that generally include core and small flake implements (Pei et al. 1958; Qiu 1985; Clark and Schick 1988; Gao 1999, 2000; Keates 2001; Gao and Norton 2002).

Since 1973 Acheulean handaxe-like stone tools have been surface collected and more recently found in situ during excavations of primary deposits in the Bose Basin in the Guangxi Zhuangzhu Autonomous Region of southern China (Huang 1987, 1989, 1993; Olsen and Miller-Antonio 1992). The heavy-duty implements are quite large, with some measuring up to 38 cm in length. Based on analysis of flake reduction and overall shape, the Bose handaxes have been found to be similar to materials from Olduvai Gorge Beds III/IV (Tanzania) and Olorgesailie (Kenya). The raw materials utilized by the Bose hominins were local quartz, quartzite, sandstone, and chert cobbles. A recent $^{40}Ar-^{39}Ar$ analysis of the associated tektites suggests an age of 803 ± 3 ka (Hou et al. 2000) for the Bose assemblage. This age makes the Bose heavy-duty stone toolkit coeval with the lithic assemblages found in the western Old World with which it shares technological similarities.

One of the most often mentioned characteristics of the East Asian bifacial implements, besides the relatively crude nature of the pieces, is how much "thicker" the tools east of the Movius Line are in relation to penecontemporaneous bifaces from Africa or the Levant (Movius 1948, 1969, 1978; Schick and Dong 1993; Clark 1994; Schick 1994). Statistical analysis was conducted on handaxes from India (Paddayya et al. 2002; Noll and Petraglia 2003; Petraglia 2005), Africa (Noll and Petraglia 2003), and Korea to test this assertion. Even though the length and width measurements did not differ statistically between the handaxe assemblages from Hunsgi-Baichbal (India), Olorgesailie (Kenya), and the HIRB (Korea), thickness does differ between regions (Tables 8-1 and 8-2). T-tests indicate significant differences between the thickness of IHRB handaxes and those from Olorgesailie and Hunsgi-Baichbal (Table 8-2).

Table 8-1. Sample sizes, means, and standard deviations of length, width, and thickness distributions of bifaces from HIRB region (Korea), Olorgesailie (Kenya), and Hunsgi-Baichbal (India) (data for Olorgesailie and Hunsgi-Baichbal biface assemblages from Noll and Petraglia, 2003: 38). Data given in mm

Locality	Smaple size	Length		Width		Thickness	
		Mean	SD	Mean	SD	Mean	SD
HIRB	58	153.86	30.46	94.16	13.92	60.19	12.92
Olorgesailie	697	161.46	41.87	93.67	19.59	41.56	10.13
Hunsgi-Baichbal	352	148.99	37.39	91.94	21.44	44.30	10.53

The variation in handaxe thickness could be a result of the original shape or the type of raw material used. Recent analysis of the handaxes fromthe Early Stone Age Isimila site (Tanzania) appears to support the assertion that the original shape of the clasts and the type of raw material are important factors in the production of more sophisticated handaxes west of the Movius Line (Bae et al. 2004), although clearly other dynamics are involved as well (Petragli, 1998). Generally, the HIRB bifaces were produced on thick river cobbles, whereas

Table 8-2. Corresponding T-scores when IHRB handaxe metric data was compared with biface assemblages from Olorgesailie (Kenya) and Hunsgi-Baichbal (India). Refer to Table 8-1 for sample sizes, means, and standard deviations for the lengths, widths, and thicknesses derived from the different handaxe assemblages used to determine the T-scores

	HIRB		
	Length	Width	Thickness
Olorgesilie	1.77	0.25	10.71*
Hunsgi-Baichbal	0.40	1.03	8.89*

those from East Africa were produced on large flakes, with a smaller percentage made on cores/clasts (Isaac 1977). HIRB bifaces were produced on quartz, quartzite, and basalt, whereas at Hunsgi-Baichbal, limestone, granite, and dolerite were used, and at Olorgesailie, basalt, phonolite, and trachyte were used (Paddayya and Petraglia 1993; Norton 2000; Noll and Petraglia 2003; see also Jones 1979). Nonetheless, in many excavations from the Indian subcontinent, refined quartz and quartzite bifaces have been recovered (Misra 1987, 1989), suggesting that raw material type alone does not dictate the overall morphology of the biface.

Even though the observed variation of the handaxe thickness east and west of the Movius Line is statistically significant, more detailed comparative analyses of the lithics are critical to developing a clearer understanding of the variation in stone toolkits across the Old World. In particular, differences between South and East Asia, which are separated by the Himalayan Mountain Range, require further study (see Petraglia 1998; Leng and Shannon 2000). For instance, analysis of flaking patterns of South and East Asian bifaces may illustrate technological variation and/or how heavily utilized certain raw materials were used in each region.

Discussion

Were East Asian hominins capable of producing sophisticated stone tools? If the stone toolkits from Bose, Dingcun, and especially those from the IHRB region in Korea (e.g., Chongokni,

Kumpari, Chuwoli, Kawoli) were included in the response to the question, then despite the apparent "thick" trait of the East Asian heavy-duty implements, and the fact that it has been noted that the Bose heavy duty tools have a higher cortical butt cortex and are unifacial, rather than bifacial (cf. Hou et al. 2000), the answer would still have to be yes. Nevertheless, after over a half-century of intensive paleoanthropological research in East Asia should we discard the Movius Line, as some have argued in the past (e.g., Yi and Clark 1983)? In the strict sense of the term, the Movius Line is not supportable (i.e. absolute presence/absence). However, if a map of East Asian Paleolithic sites were drawn, the conspicuous lack of biface-bearing sites in East Asia is still prominent, despite over 80 years of paleoanthropological research in this region of the Old World. It is not the intent here to diminish the importance of the number of East Asian Paleolithic archaeological sites that have exposed handaxes, cleavers, and picks in situ and as surface-finds.

By the Middle Pleistocene, East Asian hominins had the ability to produce sophisticated stone tools, which implies similar levels of enhanced planning aptitude and technical competence as those hominins in Africa. Nevertheless, as Movius (1944, 1948) observed over a half-century ago, East Asian Pleistocene hominins utilized different tools to carry out their everyday activities than did hominins in other regions. Three primary conclusions drawn from this study that are directly related to Movius'' observation include:

1. Compared to East Africa and India, the frequency of han-

daxe sites in East Asia is significantly lower.

2. The percentage of bifaces in these East Asian lithic assemblages is usually much lower than coeval sites from India and East Africa.
3. East Asian handaxes are not morphologically similar to typical western Old World Acheulean implements (based on thickness here, but also in other attributes and dimensions).

Upper Paleolithic Age

CHAPTER 9

Origin and patterns of the Upper Paleolithic industries in the Korean Peninsula and movement of modern humans in East Asia

Introduction

Almost 100 Upper Paleolithic sites have been discovered in the Korean peninsula, including sites of microlithic stone industries, since the first find at the Sokchangni site in the early 1960s. During the last half century, typological and chronological research of Upper Paleolithic industries has been carried out by several Paleolithic archaeologists, but few attempts have been made to understand the origin and the development processes (Norton et al. 2007). Understanding the origin of Upper Paleolithic industries in the Korean peninsula is critical for an explanation of Upper Paleolithic origins in East Asia. Also, Upper Paleolithic industries in the Korean peninsula cannot be understood without consideration of penecontemporaneous Paleolithic cultures in adjacent regions, including China, Mongolia, Siberia, and Japan.

The development of Upper Paleolithic cultures has often been discussed in relation to modern human dispersal (Mellars 1998; Klein 1999). In particular, blade technology and some human activities related to art and religion have been generally considered evidence of modern human dispersal. However, there are many parts of Eurasia where the archaeological record cannot be explained in this scheme of evolutionary processes of Upper Paleolithic culture. For example, few or no such cultural phenomena have been observed in huge areas of southeastern Asia and the southern part of mainland China. Many speculative suggestions have not provided any clear explanations of cultural patterns in this region during the Upper Paleolithic. This paper suggests that the complex pattern of the Upper Paleolithic in the Korean peninsula is derived from multiple origins, some of which have not yet been considered.

The origin of the Upper Paleolithic in the Korean peninsula is one of the most interesting cultural phenomena that contribute to reconstructions of modern human dispersal in eastern Asia. Furthermore, it provides data for understanding the patterning of human dispersal in eastern Eurasia during the last glacial period, thus contributing to a deeper understanding of modern human adaptive processes, particularly in the more remote regions of the Old World.

Stone industries and chronology

The Upper Paleolithic in the Korean peninsula is often defined by the presence of blade technology, the imported raw material of siliceous rocks, and rather extensive secondary retouching for making relatively specialized edges on small pieces (Bae 2002, 2003; Lee 2002; Norton et al. 2007). However, the boundary of the beginning of the Upper Paleolithic is still not clear, because no definite agreement has been reached on the definition of Upper Paleolithic industries. Introduction of blade technology is indisputable evidence of the beginning, as in other parts of the world. However, many stone industries without any blade technology and assemblages comprised of a mixture of blade stone tools with traditional core and flake artefacts made on quartz and quartzite materials are observed in layers which are considered to date from the latest Late Pleistocene, younger than 40,000 BP. Accordingly, assemblages classified as 'Upper Paleolithic' are diverse in their composition.

The beginning of the Upper Paleolithic in the Korean peninsula has not been well clarified and still remains to be debated. This is so because 'Upper Paleolithic' has not been defined for lithic technology, but for relative stratigraphic position of industries and chronometric dates. It has been argued that some industries without any blade technology appeared in the early stage of the Upper Paleolithic in the peninsula, hardly distinguishable from industries in the previous stage, the so called 'Middle Paleolithic'. Even local development of blade technology from the so called 'pebble tool tradition' in the previous stage, which could be called 'Middle Paleolithic' or 'Early Paleolithic', has been claimed, on the basis of presence of occasional elongate flakes which eventually developed to blade technology in the middle Upper Paleolithic Age (Lee,2005; Seong 2006a, b). However, it is hardly likely that blade technology was developed in the Korean peninsula, considering the general pattern in the Old World.

Blade technology was observed at the Sokchangni site in 1963 for the first time in the peninsula (Sohn 1967, 1978), and was ^{14}C dated to 30,690 BP. This age had been considered until recently to represent the lower boundary of the introduction of blade technology to the Korean peninsula. At present, Upper Paleolithic industries have been found in most provinces in the southern part of the peninsula (Figure 9-1). Many were found in fine sediments on riverine terraces of major river basins. Some were found in colluviums on hill slopes, and even in mountain ranges, such as the Koryeri site in the southeastern part of the Korean peninsula (Kim et al. 2002). A high density of Upper Paleolithic sites is observed in the Youngsan and Bosung river basins in the southwestern part of the peninsula. Not many blade and microblade sites have been reported in North Korea, though this is likely due to the lack of extensive archaeological research. It can be expected that many sites in the northern part of the peninsula will be reported in the future (Norton 2000). At present, the only North Korean site where Upper Paleolithic technology has been found is the Mandal cave site. Microblade cores made on

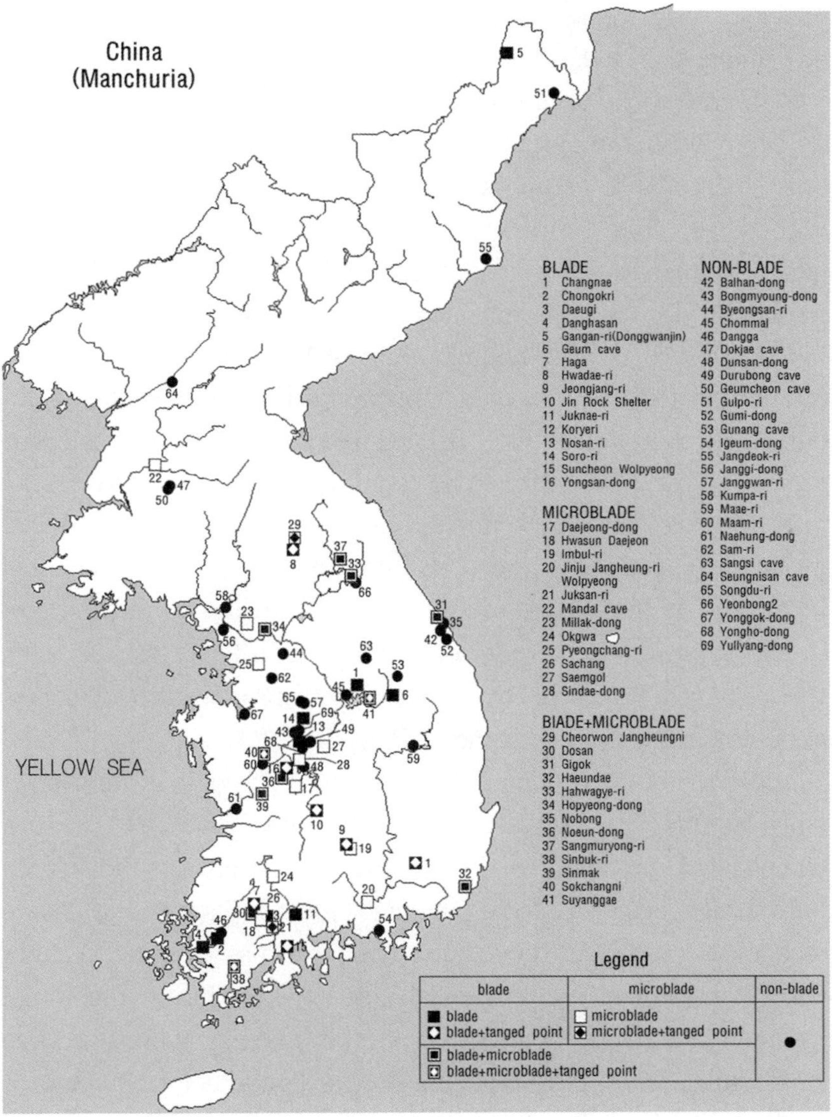

Figure 9-1. Upper Paleolithic sites on the Korean Peninsula.

obsidian were found in the cave along with anatomically modern humans, Mandal Man (Seo 1987).

Elaborate tools began to appear during the Upper Paleolithic on fine siliceous materials including end scrapers, burins, various types of side scrapers, awls, becs, and denticulates. Along with these types of tools made on blades, tools on quartz and quartzite materials are continually present even though their frequency in the assemblages decreases in the late Upper Paleolithic. It is also notable that more extensive secondary retouch on tools is observed. Tanged points appeared throughout the Upper Paleolithic. Tanged points are often considered typical Upper Paleolithic stone tools, because similar stone artefacts, the 'Hakuhen-sentoki(pointed tool on elongate flake)' in Japan, appeared in the early stage of the Upper Paleolithic industries in the Japanese archipelago (see Matsufuji 2004).

The appearance of blade technology could have been as early as 35,000 BP on the basis of current chronological evidence, although some archaeologists (e.g. Lee 2002; Seong 2006b) suggest that the beginning of the 'Upper Paleolithic' may possibly go back to between 40,000 BP and 35,000 BP. It is a complicated problem to define the beginning of the Upper Paleolithic, because some archaeologists believe that blade technology had been developed from the pre-existing technique of making elongate parallel sided flakes during the initial stage of the Upper Paleolithic in the Korean peninsula (Lee 2002; Jang 2007). It is highly probable that the introduction of blade industries is older than 30,000 BP, possibly around 35,000 BP, on the basis of ^{14}C dates (Figure 9-2).

Different systems of chronology have been attempted on the basis of frequency of fine siliceous material for tool making, technological development of blades, and geological observation of sediments and ^{14}C dates (Yi 2001; Lee 2002; Han 2003; Obata 2003; Kim et al. 2004; Seong 2006a, b). If some early industries lacking blade technology are not included, the Upper Paleolithic can be divided into two major stages on the basis

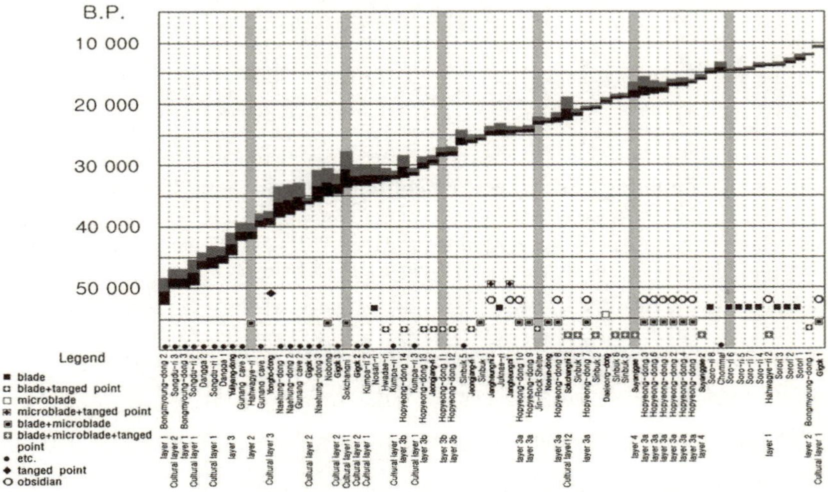

Fig. 9-2. ^{14}C dates obtained from Paleolithic sites on the Korean Peninsula.

of technological development: blades and microblades (Figure 9-3). In many Upper Paleolithic sites, these two stages appear in a series of cultural layers, but in some sites only a single stage occurs. For example, only blade tools are present at the Koryeri site, and only microblade technology at the Jangheungni site.

The early stage of the Upper Paleolithic can be represented

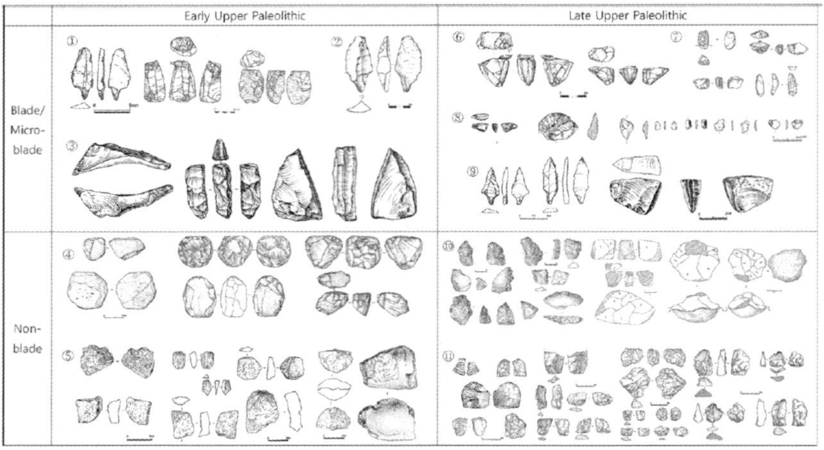

Fig. 9-3. Chronology of Upper Paleolithic industries in Korea.
(1) Koryeri; (2) Hopyeong-dong layer 1; (3) okchangni; (4) Dangga; (5) Yullyang-dong; (6) Hopyeong-dong layer 2; (7) Jangheungni; (8) Daejeong-dong; (9) Suyanggae; (10) Soro-ri; (11) Sam-ri.

by the industry from the Koryeri site in the southeastern part of the peninsula, which yielded very long and thick blades and relatively large prismatic cores with tanged points (Jang 2001). The age is not known, but is presumably earlier than 25,000 BP on the basis of the presence of possible AT tephra at the site (Seo et al. 1999). Core preparation and patterns of secondary retouch, probably similar to those from the Shuidonggou site in northern China, can be considered to represent the early stage of blade technology (Figure 9-4).

The blade industries from the Hopyeong and Deokso sites located in the Han River basin in central Korea represent the early stage of the Upper Paleolithic. The blade industry from the lower level of Hopyeong was dated between 30,000 BP and 27,500 BP (Hong and Kim 2008). The long blade stone

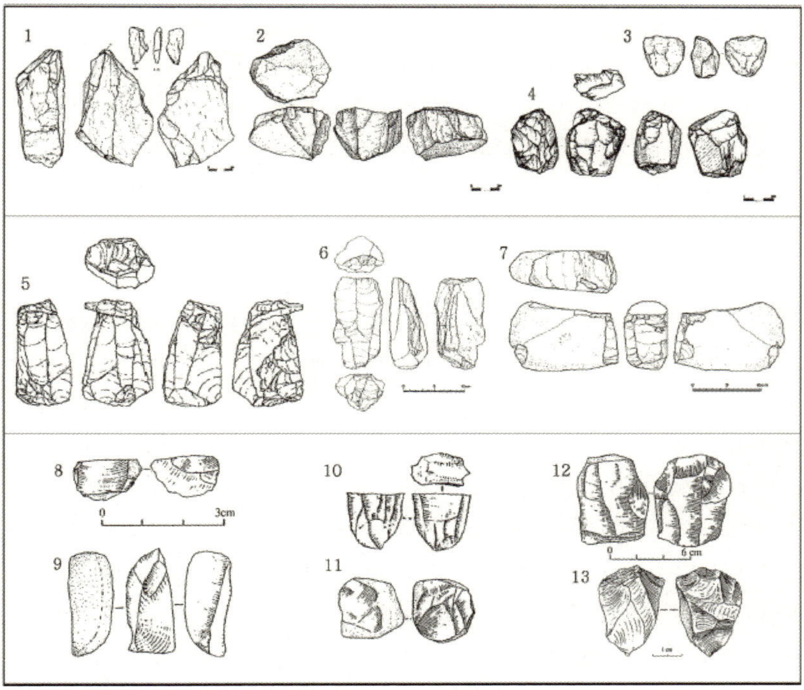

Fiure. 9-4. Cores from Deokso, Koryeri, and Shuidonggou.
(1–.4) Deokso layer 3 (Yang, 2008); (5–.7) Koryeri (Jang, 2001); (8,9) Shuidonggou locality 3; (10) layer 1 of locality 4; (11) layer 6 of locality 4; (12) locality 5 (Wang et al., 2007); (13) locality 8 (Gao et al., 2004: 313).

tools on volcanic tuff were found in association with a small flake industry on veinquartz. The AMS dates from Deokso are about 37,000 BP and 36,000 BP, which are older than those from Hopyeong. Although the Deokso dates may be considered too old, the blade cores resemble the early stage of blade technology.

Among the tool types that appeared in the early stage of the Upper Paleolithic, tanged points are a critical issue in the discussion of the beginnal of the Upper Paleolithic in Korea since the first finds at the Suyanggae site (Yi et al. 1999). A tanged point from the Yongho-dong site was found with no associations with any other blade ssiUpper Paleolithic tools. The point, recovered from the third per Paleolithi of the Yongho-dong site, was 14C AMS-dated at 38,500±1000 BP (41,926±382 {cal}; Han, 2002). This evidence is important to understanding the development of the Upper Paleolithic and the introduction of blade technology in the Korean peninsulas. Many tanged points were made on blade of fine raw material, although some were made on vein quartz, and often are assumed to be a new invention of Upper Paleolithic people. However, as the 38,500±1000 BP date is considered to be too old for the 'blade Upper Paleolithic' in Korea, additional evidence is required. Another possible explansula at some time in the terminal stage of the Middle Paleolithic, employing technology making elongate flakes, on the basis of the high frequency of its presence in the southern part of the peninsula and the very early age compared to those found in adjacent regions. The technology diffused into adjacent regions. The technology diffused int adjacent regions in cluding Japan (Masufuji 2004; Matsufuji and Okamura 1998).

Microblade technology, representing the second stage of the Upper Paleolithic, appeared ca 25 000 BP and lasted until the end of the Upper Paleolithic, persisting in some parts of the Korean peninsula into the early stage of the Neolithic. Microblade cores on obsidian at the Jangheung site in the Hantan river basin in central Korea were dated at 24 000 BP and 24 200 BP (Choi et al., 2001). In addition to this site, some early dates were obtained from the Singok site in south-western Korea (e.g. 25,420±190 BP, 25,500±1000 BP), which would be the earliest ages for microlithic industry in Korea (Lee 2004). The dates were considered somewhat older than expected in the Korean peninsula. However, the range of age dates is not extraordinary for the introduction of microlithic technology to the peninsula, considering recent evidence in China and Siberia. Some chronometric dates of microlithic sites in northern China dated older than 20,000 BP (Kuzmin 2007). Some microlithic industries in Hokkaido, Japan, are dated at 22,000 BP, and the calibrated age of the microlithic industry could be as old as 25,000 BP (Sato and Tsutsumi, 2007; Izuho and Sato, 2008). In addition, microlithic technology is believed to have appeared around 35,000 BP, long before the LGM in the Altai region, and it spread to other parts of Siberia and northeastern Asia between 30,000 BP and 20,000 BP (Derevianko 2005a, b; Kuzmin 2007).

Various types of micro-core preparation have been observed in the Korean peninsula, primarily wedge shaped cores with very few conical cores. The microlithic tradition in Korea is clearly related to that in Siberia, Inner Mongolia and northern China (Norton et al. 2007). As in the case of blades, microlithic technology has not been observed in the southern part of China, south of °35 N (Gai 1985). Even in the later part of the Upper Paleolithic in the Korean peninsula, large blades continued to appear along with microblade technology in some sites. Much more elaborate forms such as foliate bifacial points appeared in this stage, and exhaustion of cores became greater in the later part of this stage. Another change observed in microlithic industries is the absence of tanged points in industries in its final stage, which is classified as the third stage of the Upper Paleolithic by Seong (2006b). However, the terminal stage of the Upper Paleolithic and the relationship with the Neolithic culture is still unclear, although microlith and some stone tools such as arrowheads shaped by pressure techniques appeared with pottery during the incipient Neolithic culture before typical Neolithic stone tools with ground edges had appeared (Norton 2007).

The critical problem in understanding the development of Upper Paleolithic industries in Korea is the heterogeneous composition of stone artefacts and many expedient tool types with blades or microblades (Figure 9-3). Large cores of different stages, polyhedrons, choppers, and even handaxes appeared in the Upper Paleolithic. Most were made on conventional raw materials, such as quartz or quartzite cobbles, which were commonly used in the previous stage of Paleolithic culture in the peninsula. These tool types decreased when microblade technology appeared. However, they did not disappear completely anearentinued to insula. Thmade until the final stage of the Upper Paleolithic. Considering the technological efficiency of blade technology overearentinueal flake-based stone industries, simple explanations of either adaptive processes or different foraging groups do not provideeahe full picture of the Upper Paleolithic world in the peninsula. How these heterogenic characters of the Upper Paleolithic culture in the Korean peninsula can be explained is still a serious question to be answered in the future.

Origin of blade technology

Despite suggestions by some archaeologists of a local development (e.g. Lee 2005; Seong 2006a, b), blade technology in the peninsula is believed to have originated from the north, quite probably from Siberia. Blade technology in northeastern Asia is often considered to have been diffused from Siberia via the Shuidonggou site in Inner Mongolia (Matsufuji 2003, 2008; Derevianko 2005a, 2008). Current evidence shows that no other source exists except in Inner Mongolia for the introduction of blade technology in northeast China, the Korean peninsula, and the Japanese archipelago.

The blade technologies from Usti Karakol and Kara-Bom in the Altai region appear around 45,000 BP (Derevianko 2005a; Otte and Kozlowski 2005) and are believed to have diffused toward the Baikal area by around 40,000 BP. Some early Upper Paleolithic industries in the Trans-Baikal region, such as at the Podzvonkaya and Kamenka sites, were dated at least as old as 40,000 BP, and are considered similar to those found in the Altai region (Derevianko and Shunkov 2004; Lbova 2008). However, the early Upper Paleolithic in Mongolia is believed to be an archaic form, but later than in the Baikal region. Although the sediment of the second terrace of the Orkhon river bearing Upper Paleolithic industries was dated between 39,970±815 and 29,465±449 BP, conventional and AMS ^{14}C dates from Tsagaan Agui and Chikhen Agui were in the range between 34,000 BP and 26,000 BP (Derevianko and Shunkov 2004). In the Ordos region further south in Mongolia, the Shuidonggou site was uranium-series dated at 38,000±800 a. and 34,000±2000 a. However, much younger ^{14}C dates of 26,230±800 BP, 25,450±800 BP and 16,700±210 BP were obtained (Jia and Huang, 1985; Yamanaka, 1995; Matsufuji, 2003). Another set of ^{14}C dates obtained from hearth at locality 2 are placed between 29,000 and 24,000 BP (Madsen et al. 2001) and are slightly later than some dates in Korea.

Although the ^{14}C dates are younger than some early dates from blade stone industries of the Korean peninsula, the Shuidonggou site is considered the most important source in understanding the diffusion of blade technology from the Baikal region toward the Korean peninsula and other adjacent regions. As stated above, it is the only archaic form of blade technology and the oldest in the southeastern part of Asia below the latitudes of the Altai-Mongolia. Blade cores found in the Korean peninsula are similar to those from Shuidonggou. The blade cores found in the Shuidonggou site are mostly thick prismatic forms with single or double-opposite flat striking platforms made by simple retouch. Blades were detached more often from the broad sides of the cores, not from the narrow sides. This technique is considered to be an important element of the blade technology in the Altai region (Derevianko and Shunkov 2004), and is observed in the industries of major sites in the peninsula, such as

Hopyeong-dong, Deokso, Koryeri, and Sokchangni.

Important problems remain to be considered in future research concerning the origin of blade technology from Shuidonggou. At this site, blade tools were found with some Levallois elements (Jia and Huang 1985; Brantingham and Kuhn 2001) and also were mixed with microblades. Considering the fact that no true Levallois technique has been observed in China and Korea (Norton 2000; Gao and Norton, 2002 Norton et al. 2007), it is unknown at present why the Levallois technique apparently did not move further south from Inner Mongolia, while blade technology did. The route of diffusion of the blade technology from Inner Mongolia is not easy to reconstruct due to the lack of proper evidence between the Korean peninsula and Inner Mongolia. No early blade stone industry has been observed in northeast China. As is the case in North Korea, much future intensive research is required in this region including northeast China and Inner Mongolia. The current evidence from Korea indicates that blade technology diffused in a relatively short time to the northeastern part of China and the Korean peninsula. However, it did not replace the conventional types of tools on vein quartz or quartzite but coexisted along with them, as seen at some sites such as Hopyeong (Hong and Kim 2008).

Migration of modern humans and patterns of the Upper Paleolithic industries

Current human fossil evidence is hardly expected to provide any clue for the migration of modern humans into the Korean peninsula. Not many human fossils have been found in the Korean peninsula because of strong soil acidity (Norton 2000; Park and Lee 2003). With the exception of some fragmentary hominin fossils from sites in the southern part of the peninsula, most human fossils were found in limestone caves in North Korea (Chang 2002). The hominin fossils from cultural layer 2 of Yonggok cave near Pyoungyang was dated to 44,300±2000 a and 49,900±2000 a by Uranium-series dating (Kim 1991; Laboratory of Human Evolution 1995; Han 2008). These fossils show derived characters similar to modern humans. However, it was found in association with crude stone artefacts on vein quartz without any blade elements. In the Rangjeonggol cave, fragments of hominins were found in association with some crude stone artefacts. The fossils were dated between 52,000 BP and 43,000 BP by several different methods. The Mandal Man, a fully developed anatomically modern man which is considered an ancestor of modern Korean people by North Korean archaeologists, was found with obsidian microlithic industry (Chang 2002). It is the only hominin fossil that is associated with Upper Paleolithic stone industry. However, fossil evidence in the peninsula is simply not sufficient to discuss the origin of modern humans in Korea.

Both blade industries and traditional core and flake stone artefacts were present in the Upper Paleolithic in Korea. The question that arises is why Korean Upper Paleolithic peoples did not fully adopt blade technology, but, in some instances, retained core and flake tool types despite being less efficient. Does this pattern imply local evolution of blade technology, as several archaeologists have claimed (e.g. Lee 2005; Seong 2006a, b)?

The two different tool types are not likely to have been used by different groups of people. Some industries consist of purely traditional tool types on coarse quartzite or vein quartz, for example those industries from the upper layer of the Chongokni site (Bae et al. 2001). In other cases, these stone industries appeared in a mosaic pattern and were mixed in assemblages. For example, both types were found in the same layer of the Hopyeong-dong site (Hong and Kim 2008).

Why did the foraging groups who brought blade technology into the peninsula not develop it to the full? They might have adapted to the local environment in the peninsula by adopting the conventional technology of tool production instead of retaining their own tool making tradition of producing blades. Traditional core and flake tools might have been efficient enough in the environment of the Korean peninsula during the latter part of the Late Pleistocene (unlike Siberia). Furthermore, locating proper raw materials for making blades may have been more costly than simply using conventional tools along with blade tools. However, the optimal adaptation process of raw materials may not be enough to eliminate the question of why functional dominance of blade technology over traditional tools on coarse material did not appear in a general sense. Therefore, another question that needs addressing is why blade technology was not any more extensively developed after its introduction, as occurred in Siberia, in spite of the potential increase in efficiency throughout the Upper Paleolithic? Why could even much developed microblade technology not penetrate further south in China beyond the southern boundary of blade technology?

The possibility of continual influx of culture from the southern part of mainland China can be considered, along with other possible explanations such as local continuation of culture and local adaptationloct is quite likely that migration of modern humans from the southern part of mainland China continued during the late Late Pleistocene into the Korean peninsula, as in late prehistory. Foraging groups in southern China had only conventional tools throughout the Paleolithic Age (Wang 1997, 2004; Matsufunji 2003). Flake-based stone industries in the southern part of China would have provided modern humans sufficient tools to survive in the region, even during the Last Glacial Maxium. Population growth would have been sufficient to extend to the Hwangha river basin, where the southern boundary of blade technology lies, and possibly further north. No element of blade technology has been observed in the Upper Paleolithic industries from Zhououdian upper cave (Zhang and Pei 1985; Norton and Gao 2008) and Xiaogushan in northeastern China.

Humans likely migrated into the Korean peninsula through the exposed Yellow Sea basin during glacial periods, continuously bringing their flake-based stone industries to the peninsula, mixing with blade stone industries. However, the environment was probably not so severe for those populations from both directions to change their technology during the early stage of Upper Paleolithic, and even in the late part of the Upper Paleolithic when they frequently used blade-based stone industries and microblade stone industries. The 'heterogenic' pattern of stone industries is often explained as conservatism in tool production in the Upper Paleolithic Age in Korea. However, persistence over such a long time as a general pattern needs another model of explanation. This 'North-South model' of Upper Paleolithic pattern in East Asia might even be helpful to explain why no true Levallois technique has been observed in mainland China and Korea. At the time of the 'Middle Paleolithic', the northern boundary of the flake-based industries moved northward andwas probably dominant in most of China and Korea, even in northern China. This is not simply a cultural pattern, but a representation of direction of human migration at that time. Homo sapiens or modern humans with flake-based tools, but without any Levallois technique, possibly expanded their territory further north in the 'Middle Paleolithic'.

Further evidence may be needed to support this idea, such as comparative analysis of stone industries and human fossils. However, the current general pattern of distribution of blade stone industries in this region and two eastward migration routes of modern Homo sapiens in the Eurasian continent should be considered as concrete grounds for the explanation of the 'heterogenic'origin of the Upper Paleolithic industries in the Korean peninsula (Figure 9-5). In the north, a group of modern humans brought blade technology via Altai and Mongolia to the Korean peninsula, while another group of people from southern China migrated to the peninsula with conventional industries lacking blade technology. The North-South model of Upper Paleolithic migrations could also be supported by the general pattern of Paleolithic industries in the Japanese archipelago. In the early stage of the Upper Paleolithic, two different tool technologies have been proposed in the northern and southern parts of the Japanese archipelago. Well developed blade-based stone industries appeared in

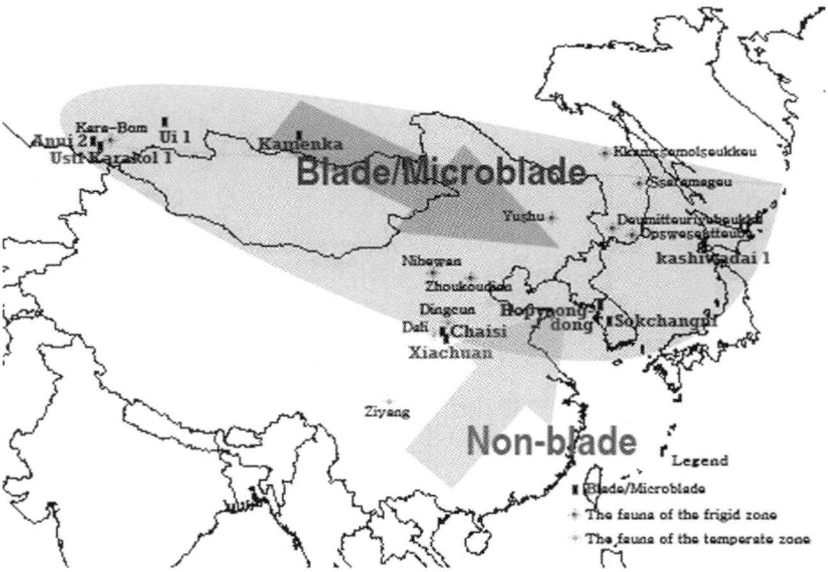

Figure 9-5. Boundary of distribution of blade/microblade industries in East Asia.

northeastern Japan, while flake-based stone industries are common in southwestern Japan (Sato 2008).

It has been a common understanding that modern Homo

came into the Korean peninsula from Siberia not only in the historical period but even in the Upper Pleistocene. However, modern human migration from southern China to northeast China or even to the Korean peninsula has also been proposed by Chinese geneticists on the basis of the analysis of Y-chromosomes (Hong et al. 2005). According to the analysis, the O3-M122 haplotype is believed to have originated from southern East Asia, due to a higher frequency of polymorphisms than in northeastern Asia. Hong et al. (2005) concluded that early northward migration of the O3-M122 lineage in East Asia occurred 30,000-25,000 BP. Regardless of the time of the early boundary, this genetic study of modern Asians supports anatomically modern human migration from southern China toward the Korean Peninsula and northeastern China during the late pa rt of the Upper Paleolithic, which provides support for the 'North and South model' of human migrations with different Paleolithic cultures. Previous genetic studies also support the theory that the prevailing gene flow had been in a south-to-north direction before the Holocene when bidirectional gene flow possibly occurred (Karafet et al. 2001; Su et al. 1999).

Conclusion

The 'heterogenic' origin of the Upper Paleolithic industries in the Korean peninsula can be explained by the "North and South model" of modern human migrations. Modern humans dispersing from western Siberia toward Mongolia and eastern Siberia brought blade technology to the Korean peninsula and also to the northern part of the Japanese archipelago, while modern human populations equipped with conventional flake industries from southern China continually migrated toward the northeastern part of East Asia, including the Korean peninsula. Migrations of modern human populations of the two origins were merged in the Korean peninsula and resulted in the heterogenic Upper Paleolithic cultures. Human dispersal into far eastern asia is observed more clear from two direction in north and south in late upper pleistocene while it was ob-scure due to few supporting evidence for hominine movement in unfavorable environment of eastern siberia. More extensive survey in this region is expected to provide evidence support-ing northern movement before upper paleolithic.

The mixture of the two quite different technologies cannot be explained by mixtures of modern humans with those of the previous evolutionary stage as suggested by some Korean archaeologists. Rather, different modern human populations with different cultures came to the peninsula and kept their tool making tradition for a time after their arrival, along with maintaining the local tradition of tool making. Population in-flux from the south might have been much greater than that from the north into the Korean peninsula and conventional flake-based industries prevailed even in the late period, al-though blade technology was more frequent and dominant in particular assemblages. Northward migration from southern China during the late Upper Pleistocene is supported by genetic analysis of the modern population's Y-chromosome in this area. This model of human migration may be helpful to our understanding of the Upper Paleolithic patterns in the Japanese archipelago where blade technology was absent in the southwestern part of the archipelago in the early stage of the Upper Paleolithic until blade technology was diffused in the later period.

The region between the Korean peninsula and Inner Mongolia needs to be investigated to better understand the movement of modern humans during the Upper Paleolithic. However, the Korean blade technology is believed to have moved from the north, quite possibly via Inner Mongolia where the Shuidonggou site is situated. At present, blade technology is considered to have been introduced into the peninsula at a time evidently earlier than 30,000 BP and possibly 35,000 BP. It is interesting to note that microblade technology expanded further south than blade technologies in China, possibly due to climatic factors, but never reached South China.

CHAPTER 10

The nature of the Early to Late Paleolithic transition in Korea: Current perspectives

Introduction

In eastern Asia, the transition from the Early to Late Paleolithic is only slowly becoming better realized (Gao and Norton 2002; Norton and Jin 2009; Norton et al. 2009). Norton and Jin (2009) recently reviewed the East Asian record (restricted to China, Korea, and Japan) and found that more evidence for the saltational model of modern human behavior exists in the north, while the archaeological record in the south appears to support more of a gradualistic model. The saltational model, as defined by Norton and Jin (2009: 247) states that "between 50 and 40 kya modern human behavior appears suddenly and as a "package"; that is, the entire range of traits appeared more or less simultaneously". The gradualistic model suggests that modern human behaviors appeared intermittently, gradually building up over long periods of time (Norton and Jin 2009). The earliest evidence for the transition to the Late Paleolithic (e.g. introduction of blade and micro-blade technologies) appears in northern China, Korea, and Japan. It is currently not clear about when the evidence of modern human behavior begins to appear in Southeast Asia (including southern China).However, there is currently an absence of evidence of blade and microblade technologies in Late Pleistocene Southeast Asia (Norton and Jin 2009). Interestingly, the archaeological record currently conflicts with some genetic studies that argue for modern humans arriving initially in southern China and dispersing northward (for discussion, see Su et al. 1999; Jin and Su 2000; Karafet et al. 2001; Shi et al. 2005; Norton and Jin 2009; Di and Sanchez-Mazas 2011 and below). It should be noted that Shea (2011) recently suggested that paleoanthropologists may be overemphasizing the presence/absence of blades/microblades to argue for presence/absence of "modern human behavior". Indeed, recent studies in Africa (Johnson and McBrearty 2010) and the Levant (Shimelmitz et al. 2011) indicate that blade technology may ctually well predate the evolution ofmodern Homosapiens (McDougall et al. 2005). Although Shea (2011)was referring to the western Old World, it is interesting that blades/microblades do not appear in Southeast Asia, including southern China, but that some genetics studies argue for the initial appearance of modern humans in that region and later migrations into northern China (e.g., Su et al. 1999; Jin and Su 2000; Shi et al. 2005). If it is true that modern humans arrived first in southern China and they had what might be considered "modern human" behavior, then they clearly did so without needing to rely on blade stone tool technology. This may provide indirect support for Shea's (2011) suggestion that paleoanthropologists may be overstating the relationship between blade stone tool technology and "modern human behavior." There is a paucity of clear evidence of a distinct "Middle" Paleolithic in eastern Asia (Ikawa-Smith 1978; Norton 2000; Gao and Norton 2002; Bae 2002b; Norton et al. 2009; Seong 2009). Indeed, KD Bae (2002b: 473) writes "following Western archaeological practices, the Korean Paleolithic is divided into three substages, the Lower, Middle, and Upper Paleolithic.

However, there are few clear changes in stone industries between so-called Early and Middle Paleolithic industries, bringing into question the utility of these designations." In this paper we utilize a two stage classification system: Early and Late Paleolithic (Gao and Norton 2002). It should be noted however that many Korean (and Chinese and Japanese) Paleolithic specialists continue to use a three stage cultural sequence (Lower, Middle, Upper) indiscriminately without clearly defining what they mean by a distinct "Middle Paleolithic" (but see Yoo 2007). Although it is beyond the cope of the current paper to evaluate this question, we strongly recommend this is a question that should be taken up by Korean (and Chinese and Japanese) Paleolithic researchers in the future. In other words, the questions should be framed as:

1) "exactly how is the "Middle" Paleolithic being defined in eastern Asia?"; and 2) "is it useful to continue to apply the western three stage Paleolithic theoretical framework to the eastern Asian record?" (Gao and Norton 2002; Norton et al. 2009; Norton and Jin 2009; Seong 2009; for discussion about theoretical aspects of what modern human behavior actually represents see recent papers by; McBrearty and Brooks 2000; Henshilwood and Marean 2003; Mellars et al. 2007; Shea 2011). In answer to the above questions, a detailed evaluation by Gao and Norton (2002) drew the conclusion that: 1) the "Middle" Paleolithic is currently poorly defined in eastern Asia; and 2) the three stage Paleolithic cultural sequence (Lower, Middle, Upper) developed for the western Old World, particularly Europe, is currently not an appropriate model to use for the eastern Asian record (see also Norton et al. 2009; Seong 2009). Thus, in this paper we use the two stage (Early and Late) Paleolithic sequence.

The nature of the Early to Late Paleolithic transition in Korea is still poorly understood (Seong 2006, 2009; Bae 2010; Lee 2011). In general, the Korean Early Paleolithic is represented by a combination of core and flake tools, usually produced on locally available quartz and quartzite, with the occasional presence of a small bifacial component (Bae 1988; Norton 2000; Yoo 2007).

Good examples of the latter artifact composition are many of the sites located in the HIRB (Bae 1988, 1994, 2002a; Norton 2000; Norton et al. 2006; Yoo 2007; Norton and Bae 2009). One of the interesting aspects of the Korean Late Paleolithic is that some stone toolkits continue to be comprised of typical Early Paleolithic core and flake tools, while other lithic assemblages are comprised of blade and microblade stone tools (Bae and Kim 2003; Norton et al. 2007a; Seong 2007, 2009; Bae 2010; Lee 2011). This interesting characteristic of the Korean Late Paleolithic has been explained by indigenous behavioral evolution (Seong 2006, 2009). For instance, Seong (2009: 417) recently stated that "Late Paleolithic technological characteristics emerged ca. 40,000–30,000 BP, but not until the onset of the OIS 2 did formal artifacts, such as blades and blade tools, became sic predominant in lithic assemblages. This change is viewed as a slow, evolutionary process that eventually culminated in the Late Paleolithic transition." The other major proposed model to explain this behavioral transition in Korea is a combination of different foraging groups emigrating from Siberia and southern China (aka "North-South model"; Bae 2010).

The focus of this synthesis is to evaluate these two models. In particular, we review the nature of the archaeological and hominin fossil records during the marine isotope stage (MIS) 3–2 transition (~40–25 ka), particularly in its paleoenvironmental setting (Figure 10–1; Table 10–1). Based on current evidence in Korea, this is the period when the Early to Late Paleolithic transition occurs and a time when the climate shifts from a relatively warm to a colder environment. The environmental framework is particularly important because neither of the earlier models (but see Seong (2008) for some discussion) appeared to place much importance on it. Although it is diffi-

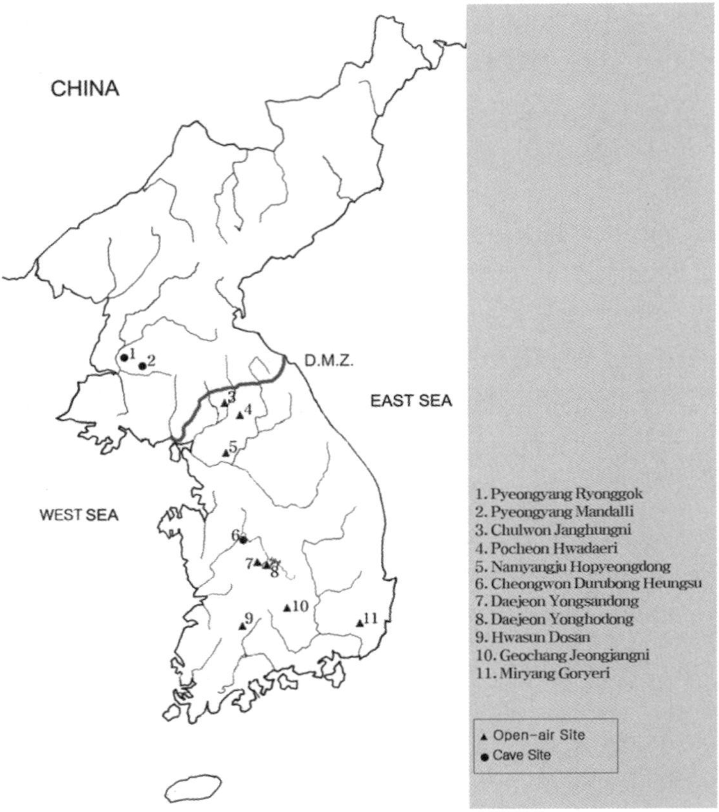

Figure 10-1. Locations of sites mentioned in text.

Table 10-1. Korean sites discussed in text. Location # represents site position in Figure 10-1.

Location	Name	Open Air/Cave	Sample Position	Age (dating method)	Artefacts	Hominin Fossils	Reference
1	Ryonggok	Cave		500-400 ka(TL) 48-46 ka (U-series)		Yes	Jun et al. 1986; Norton 2000; CJ Bae 2010
2	Mandali	Cave		20,000 BP		Yes	Kim et al. 1985; KD

							Bae 2010
3	Janghungni	Open Air	Light brown layer Light brown layer	24,200 ± 600 (AMS) 24,400 ± 600 (AMS)	Yes	No	Choi et al. 2001
4	Hwadaeri	Open Air	1st cultural layer	22,000 ± 1000 (OSL)	Yes	No	Choi 2007
			2nd cultural layer	33,680 ± 1009 (calibrated AMS)			Choi and Ryu 2005; Choi 2007
			3rd cultural layer	39,000 ± 1400(OSL)			Choi 2007
5	Hopyeongdong	Open Air	Brown sandy clay(northeastern part of the site	16,190 ± 50 (AMS) 16,900 ± 500 (AMS) 16,600 ± 720 (AMS) 17,500 ± 400 (AMS) 17,400 ± 400 (AMS) 15,000 ± 1100 (OSL)	Yes	No	Hong and Kim 2008
			Brown sandy clay (western part of site)	21,100 ± 200(AMS) 22,200 ± 200 (AMS) 23,900 ± 400 (AMS) 24,100 ± 200 (AMS)			
			Dark brown	27,600 ± 300(AMS) 27,500 ± 300 (AMS) 29,200 ± 900 (AMS) 30,000 ± 1500 (AMS)			
			Colluvial	8 dates between 34,500 ± 800 and 31,000 ± 500 (AMS)	one vein quartz core		
6	Heungsu (Turubong)	Cave		12,100 ± 130 (AMS)	No	Yes	Seoul National University AMS laboratory n.d.
7	Yongsandong	Open Air	Brownish clay layer	24,430 ± 870 (AMS)	Yes	No	JRICH 2007
8	Yonghodong	Open Air	Light brown layer	38,500 ± 1000 (AMS)	Yes	No	Han 2002
9	Dosan	Open Air	Sandy clay containing bedrok fragments (first)	61,380 ± 3040 (OSL)	Yes	No	Lee and Kim 2009; Lee 2011
			Yellowish brown sandy clay (second)	53,000 ± 4110 (OSL)			
			Dark brown clay with soil wedge	46,080 ± 1720 (OSL)			

10	Jeongjangni	Open Air	(third) Light brown clay (fourth) Dark brown soil layer	28,100 ± 1950 (OSL) 25,700 ± 150 29,200 ± 900 29,760 ± 300 28,600 ± 300 26,300 ± 1100 29,340 ± 700 3,060 ± 40 22,100 ± 300 33,500 ± 1200	Yes	No	Gyeongnam Development Institute 2004
11	Goryeri	Open Air		Below the AT tephra (~25-22 ka)	Yes	No	Jang 2001; Kim et al. 2002

cult to necessarily associate a specific hominin taxon with a specific stone tool type [e.g. see difficulties with trying to determine who the first stone toolmakers were (Toth and Schick 2009)], it will still be a useful exercise to see if pertinent variation is present in the hominin fossil record. The same applies to the behavioral record. In other words, does the transition fromthe Early to Late Paleolithic represent a "slow, evolutionary process" as proposed by Seong (2009: 417) or a combination of different foraging groups dispersing into the Korean Peninsula from the north and the south as proposed by KD Bae (2010)? What should be evident from this review is that currently, the Korean hominin fossil record offers relatively little to addressing this transition, while the Paleolithic record indicates that a major behavioral transition occurred during this period. Both Seong (2009) and KD Bae (2010) are correct in a number of aspects of their models. However, we add a few more relevant points which we believe will help to better understand the nature of the Early to Late Paleolithic transition in Korea.

Paleolithic archaeology record

The boundary of the beginning of the Upper Paleolithic in Korea is still not clear, because no definite agreement has been reached on the definition of Upper Paleolithic industries. Introduction of blade technology is indisputable evidence of the beginning, as in other parts of the world. However, many stone industries without any blade technology and assemblages comprised of a mixture of blade stone tools with traditional core and flake artefacts made on quartz and quartzite materials are observed in layers which are considered to date from the latest Late Pleistocene, younger than 40,000 BP. Accordingly, assemblages classified as 'Upper Paleolithic' are diverse in their composition(Bae 2010: 104).

In general, the Korean Late Paleolithic can be divided into two cultural stages: 1) an initial blade technology that appears sometime between 40 and 35 ka; and 2) around 25 ka microblades begin to appear in the archaeological record (Figure 10-2; Seong 2009; Bae 2010). Because the focus of our paper is the MIS 3-2 transition, we restrict our discussion to sites that have been dated to around 40-25 ka. Reviews of Korean Late Paleolithic sites that date to around or postdate the Last Glacial Maximum appear elsewhere (e.g. KD Bae and Kim 2003; Norton et al. 2007a; Seong 2007, 2008, 2009; KD Bae 2010; Lee 2011). A handful of sites currently exist in Korea that have been dated to the MIS 3-2 transition by AMS

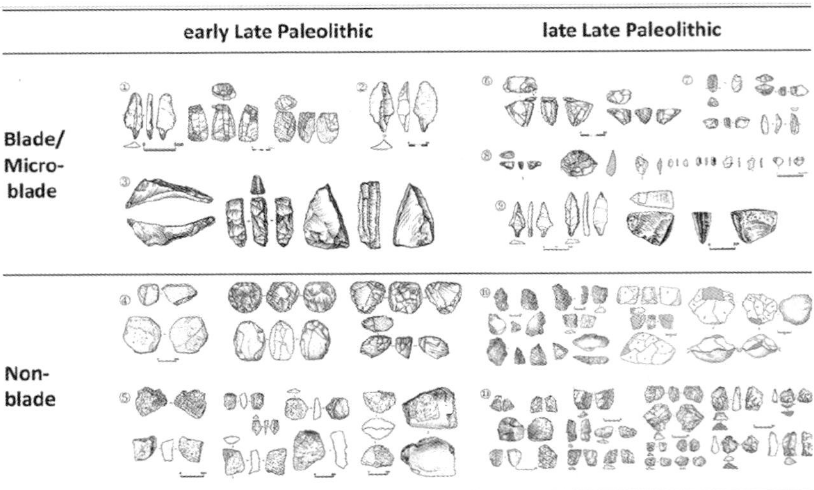

Figure 10-2. Examples of lithics from the early and late Late Paleolithic. (Modified from KD Bae, 2010: his Figure 3).

(1) Goryeri; (2) Hopyeongdong layer 1; (3) Sokchangni; (4) Dangga; (5) Yullyang-ong; (6) Hopyeongdong layer 2; (7) Jangheungni; (8)Daejeongdong; (9) Suyanggae; (10) Sorori; (11) Samri.

and/or optically stimulated minescence (OSL) dating methods (Bae 2002b, 2010; KD Bae and Kim 2003; Seong 2009; CJ Bae and Kim 2010; Lee 2011). these include, but are not restricted to Yonghodong, Hwadaeri, Hopyeongdong, Yongsandong, Janghungni, Jeongjangni, and Goryeri, all located in present day South Korea. Many other Late Paleolithic sites have been identified throughout South Korea, though most still do not have secure chronometric dates or have been intensively studied (e.g., see Lee 2011 of his recent review of the Paleolithic of the Honam region of southwestern Korea where more than 300 Paleolithic sites were found). As we have noted elsewhere (e.g. Norton 2000; CJ Bae 2010), due to the sociopolitical climate of North Korea, it is difficult to synthesize recent paleo-anthropological findings identified in that region.

Although it falls outside the scope of the present paper, we do discuss the important North Korean Late Paleolithic Mandalli site.

We review each of these sites below in rough chronological order (see also, KD Bae, 2002a; b, 2010; Norton et al., 2007a; Seong, 2007, 2009). Because chronologies change fairly frequently, we describe these sites in chronological order based on the generally accepted dates at the time of this writing. Yonghodong is an open-air site located near Daejon in central South Korea. The site contains four cultural horizons with various core and flake tools present throughout the stratigraphic sequence (Han 2002). At least one tanged point was found in each of the second and third stratigraphic layers. A sample of charcoal found in he third cultural level was AMS dated to 38,500 ± 1000 BP (41,926 ± 382 {cal}; Han 2002), which would suggest that the tanged point that derives from the third layer is coeval with the charcoal. The calibrated age of the tanged point would push the boundary of the Early to Late Paleolithic transition in Korea back to more than 40,000 BP (see Norton and Jin 2009; CJ Bae and Kim 2010; KD Bae 2010 for discussion and possible implications). However, others (e.g. Seong 2009; KD Bae 2010) have suggested it is too early to draw any conclusions regarding the Yonghodong tanged point because it is a single artifact (possibly originating from he second cultural horizon, which also has a tanged point?) and it is only one date. We agree that additional dating analyses and more research regarding the relationship between the tanged point and the charcoal are necessary to help clarify the importance of the Yonghodong findings. Hwadaeri is an open-air site located in Kangwon Province along a tributary of the Hantan River (Choi and Ryu 2005). Three stratigraphic levels were identified with a series of OSL analyses indicating that the first stratigraphic level dates to 22,000 ± 1000 BP, the middle horizon to 30,000 ± 1700 BP, and the lowermost stratigraphic level to 39,000 ± 1400 BP (Choi and Ryu 2005; CJ Bae and Kim 2010). A charcoal sample derived from the middle horizon was AMS dated to 31,200 ± 900 BP, which corroborates the OSL date. More than 5000 artifacts were found throughout the profile (Choi and Ryu 2005; Seong 2009). The lowermost horizon exposed artifacts comprised primarily of core and flake tools produced on locally available vein quartz and quartzite. However, the second stratigraphic level revealed the presence of a small percentage of blades and tanged points produced on porphyry, a higher quality raw material. Blades and smaller flake tools were excavated from the first horizon, but as with the second stratum, represent only a small percentage of the overall lithic assemblage (Choi and Ryu 2005; Seong 2009).

Hopyeongdong is an open-air site located in the central region of South Korea. Seven stratigraphic layers were identified,with cultural materials found in two separate horizons within the third stratigraphic layer (Hong and Kim 2008). An abundance of charcoal samples were collected for AMS dating analysis. The chronometric studies indicated that the lower stratigraphic level ranged in age between 30,000 ± 1500 BP and 27,600 ± 300 BP, while the upper cultural horizon could be bracketed between 24,100 ± 200 BP and 21,1000 ± 200 BP (Hong and Kim 2008). The artifact assemblage from the lower cultural horizon includes blades and tanged points that were produced primarily on siliceous shale and tuff. The upper cultural layer contains microblades and microblade cores produced on obsidian. In a different area of the site, microblades and microblade cores produced on siliceous shale were found with AMS dates ranging between 17,400 ± 400 BP and 16,190 ± 50 BP (Hong and Kim 2008; Seong 2009; KD Bae 2010). The Hopyeongdong blades appear to be penecontemporaneous with or slightly younger than the Hwadaeri materials. As with the Hwadaeri materials, blades and microblades represent only a relatively small proportion of the overall lithic assemblage.

Dosan is an open-air site located outside of Kwangju in the southwestern part of the Korean peninsula. Four Paleolithic horizons were identified during excavations with more than 5000 artifacts recovered (Lee 2002, 2011; Lee and Kim 2009). A series of OSL dates were analyzed on samples collected from the various strata. The age range is 61,380 ± 3000 BP from layer 1 to 28,100 ± 1950 BP from layer 4. One of the interesting aspects of the Dosan site is the presence of the typical eastern Asian Early Paleolithic core and flake stone tool industry in the older stratigraphic levels and the introduction of blades in the youngest stratum (layer 4). Most of the artifacts from Dosan are produced on locally available quartz and quartzite, but better quality rhyolite appears in layer 4, not surprisingly, coinciding with the introduction of blades (Lee, 2011).

A number of sites in Korea have been dated to around the beginning of MIS 2. Some of the best described are the open-air sites of Yongsandong, Goryeri, and Janghungni (Seong 2009; KD Bae 2010). All of these sites' lithic assemblages are represented by increasing frequencies in blade and/or the introduction of microblades. Yongsandong is an open-air site located in Daejon. More than 2,300 lithic artefacts were excavated from the brownish clay with soil cracks, including 233 blades and 37 tanged points. A soil sample taken from the brownish clay layer resulted in an AMS date of 24,430 ± 870 BP (JRICH 2007). In Korea, the presence of soil cracks in the stratigraphy is usually interpreted to represent deposits laid down during the Last Glacial Maximum (Kim and Lee 2006). Excavations at the open-air site of Goryeri in Miryang in southeastern Korea revealed the presence of a diversity of blades.

Although AT tephra was identified in the overlying horizon, no chronometric dates exist for the Goryeri blades (KD Bae 2010). Fairly clear evidence of the relationship between the advent of microblade technologies in Korea and the onset of MIS 2 is the microblade assemblage excavated from Janghungni, an open-air site from Cheolwon, in Kangwon Province. The microblade collection was excavated from the second stratigraphic level with two associated AMS dates of 24,200 ± 600 BP and 24,400 ± 600 BP (Choi et al. 2001). It should be noted that calibrating these dates will actually push them back to the terminal stage of MIS 3 (~27,000 cal. BC), which would be a very early date for the initial appearance of microlithics in eastern Asia. Microblades from the Sinbuk site in southwestern Korea also have older dates (25,420 ± 190 BP; 25,500 ± 1000 BP) (Lee 2004; Lee and Kim 2008), that if calibrated would also predate the beginning of MIS 2 by several thousand years.

Hominin fossil record

The Korean hominin fossil record is relatively sparse for this time period (Park 1992; Norton 2000; CJ Bae 2010). In part, this is due to the highly acidic soil in Korea that hinders bone preservation and fossilization at almost all open-air sites other than shell middens. It is also due to the lack of systematic surveys of the hundreds of caves present in the limestone mountainous regions that make up much of the peninsula (CJ Bae and KD Bae n.d.). Two cave sites in North Korea (Ryonggok, Mandalli) and one cave locality in South Korea (Heungsu Turubong) do exist and have been relatively well researched (Figure 10-2; Table 10-1).

Ryonggok is arguably the most important hominin bearing site on the Korean Peninsula (Norton 2000; CJ Bae 2010). It is located just outside the North Korean capital city of Pyeongyang (Jun et al. 1986; CJ Bae 2010). A diversity of hominin fossils representing at least five individuals were excavated from four separate stratigraphic layers. The fossils were originally assigned to archaic H. sapiens, based primarily on an initial thermoluminescence date of 500,000–400,000 BP. However, later uranium-series dates placed the material around 48,000–46,000 BP and more detailed study of the morphology of the crania, including cranial capacities of 1,450 ㎤ and 1,650 ㎤ and the presence of a mental eminence on the associated mandibles suggest an early modern H. sapiens designation might be more appropriate (CJ Bae 2010). Because the mandibles clearly represent older individuals, it was recently suggested that the site may have served as a burial site (CJ Bae 2010).

Geometric morphometric analyses would help to clarify the taxonomic assignment of the Ryonggok hominin fossils and more detailed evaluation of the site and associated archaeology could clarify the possibility of the site having served as a burial locality.

Mandalli is a cave site located along the Taedong River 20 km east of Pyeongyang (Kim et al. 1985; Norton 2000; CJ Bae 2010). KD Bae (2010) cites an age of 20,000 BP, while based on the biostratigraphy (e.g. *Cervus nippon, Vulpes vulpes, Hyaena sp.*) and associated archaeology the site has been dated to around the Late Pleistocenee Holocene (Norton 2000; Norton et al. 2007a). Three stratigraphic levels were identified, with Neolithic artifacts (e.g. Chulmun pottery sherds, worked bone tools), found in the uppermost layer. Human fossils were found in the second horizon along with a small sample of obsidian tools (microcore blades and bladelets). The third stratigraphic level revealed only vertebrate paleontological materials

(Norton et al. 2007a). The human fossil assemblage includes a partial cranium, two partial mandibles, and a partial humerus representing at least two modern humans (Kim et al. 1985; Park 1992; Norton 2000). It should be noted that published mesialedistal and buccalelingual measurements of two lower second molars associated with the human fossils falls within the range of older archaic hominins (CJ Bae 2010). As with the Ryonggok materials, little more can be currently said about Mandalli because of the irregular access to information about the paleoanthropology of North Korea (Norton 2000). However, Mandalli is one of the most important sites in Korea because relatively few sites have exposed the full range of materials (e.g. hominin fossils, vertebrate paleontology, and stone artifacts) necessary to addressing paleoanthropological debates (Norton 2000; CJ Bae 2010).

Heungsu Cave is one of several caves that make up the Turubong cave complex (Park and Lee 1990; Park 1992; Norton 2000). The site is important due to the discovery of a modern H. sapiens child skeleton that is thought to have been interred. Heungsu child, as it is commonly referred to as, is a fairly intact skeleton with an almost complete cranium and most of the postcrania present. Based on tooth eruption the child is thought to have been about 5e6 years old at the time of death (Park and Lee 1990; Park 1992). The age of the interment is thought to have been about 40,000 BP, based on the initial biostratigraphy studies. However, the relationship between the human skeleton and the associated faunas has been questioned, with the possibility that the Heungsu child is a more recent intrusive burial (Norton 2000). Indeed, AMS dates on associated charcoal samples indicated a much more recent age (12,100 ± 130 BP; 10,390 ± 80 BP), though it should be noted that the relationship between the charcoal samples and the human skeleton is unclear.

Discussion

Various models have been suggested to explain the transition from the Early to Late Paleolithic in Korea. For instance, it is possible that the behavioral transitionwas an in situ evolutionary event (e.g. Seong 2006). It is also possible that the transition represents migrations into the peninsula from blade/microblade carrying foraging groups from the north and core/flake carrying foraging groups from the south (e.g. KD Bae 2010). Yet, a third possibility is that blade/microblade using foraging groups in the north interacted with the indigenous hominins already present in the Korean peninsula area between MIS 3-2 and the slow but increasing frequency of blades and microblades in stone toolkits, particularly after ~25,000 BP, reflect this. We evaluate each of these models in turn.

In situ evolution model

Seong (2009) argues that the best documentation for the Early to Late Paleolithic transition in Korea is fromthe evidence of larger core and flake tools, which are found in older deposits, and blade and microblades, which are found either in overlying stratigraphic layers or in younger deposits at other sites. According to Seong (2006), the increasing frequency of blades in these sites is evidence for an in situ evolutionary development. However, one of us has argued elsewhere that if a true in situ evolutionary behavioral transition occurs, then we should anticipate seeing a transition from Mode I (Oldowan) to Mode II (Acheulean) to Mode III (Levallois) to Mode IV (Blades) to Mode V (Microblades) lithic technologies (Lycett and Bae 2010; Lycett and Norton 2010). Currently the only region of the Old World where we see such a continuous evolutionary development is Africa (Lycett and Bae 2010; Lycett and Norton 2010). Indeed, the clear absence of the Levallois technology in much of eastern Asia until the MIS 3-2 transition (Gao and Norton 2002; Norton et al. 2009), should be good evidence that eastern Asia is probably not a region where we see many clear in situ behavioral evolutionary developments during the Pleistocene. The supposed evolutionary transition" from Mode I core and flake tools directly to Mode IV and V blade and microblade industries in Korea (e.g. Hwadaeri, Dosan) should make this point fairly evident. In our view, absence of such continuous behavioral evolutionary transitions during much of the Pleistocene in eastern Asia suggests lower population densities and bottlenecks (during the earlier part of the Pleistocene) and population movements and/or interactions (during the latter part of the Pleistocene) rather than a slow continuous evolutionary development that resulted in major shifts in the lithic technologies (for discussion see also Gao and Norton 2002; KD Bae 2010; Lycett and Bae 2010; Lycett and Norton 2010).

On a related note regarding the Seong (2008, 2009) argument, is that there is something to be said about making arguments about hominin subsistence patterns through the presence of certain types of stone tools. Indeed, Shea (2007: 226) recently justifiably observed that "recognizing the role that variability may have played in Early Paleolithic stone-tool design is a significant step toward more realistic models of early hominin subsistence". Nevertheless, we find Seong's (2009) recent attempt at correlating changes in human subsistence strategies with changes in lithic technology in Late Pleistocene Korea somewhat lacking in empirical support. Seong (2008: 881) draws two primary conclusions from his review of the Korean Late Paleolithic record: 1) presence of a tanged point "suggests hunting activities were widely practiced during the early Late Palaeolithic;" and 2) later a heavier reliance on microliths, that were supposedly used to hunt small animals and birds. Nevertheless, as Shea (2006: 842) notes, "evidence for effective big game hunting long precedes the widespread use of projectile weaponry."

There is a diversity of studies from the geosciences and archaeology that support the argument that late Middle and early Late Pleistocene Neanderthal and archaic H. sapiens foraging groups were already proficient hunters, well before the advent of projectile technology (e.g. Marean and Kim 1998; Richards et al. 2000; Norton and Gao 2008a; contra Seong

2008). There is a plethora of taphonomic literature readily available that strongly suggests that detailed evaluation of associated vertebrate paleontological remains can be much more informative than studying associated lithics to reconstruct hominin hunting prowess (or lack thereof) (e.g. Binford 1981, 1984; Blumenschine and Marean 1993; Blumenschine 1995; Blumenschine and Pobiner 2006). Indeed, there is a growing body of taphonomic studies from East Asia that provide ample evidence for early hominin hunting strategies during the Early Paleolithic or into the Late Paleolithic (e.g. Norton and Gao 2008a, b; Norton et al. 2010a). Other recent taphonomic studies from the region have actually raised questions about archaeologists' interpretations of purported hominin kill sites (e.g. Norton et al. 2007b). Thus, vertebrate taphonomic studies should receive priority when trying to determine how effective early hominin hunting strategies may have been or when we begin to see a shift from less effective to more effective procurement patterns.

North-South [Migration] Model

One of us (KD Bae) recently proposed a new model to challenge the idea that the Early to Late Paleolithic transition in Korea occurred as an in situ evolutionary event. This model is referred to as the "North-South [Migration] Model" (KD Bae 2010). The basic premise that underlies the North-South Migration Model is that Paleolithic foragers continued to be mobile up until the very end of the Terminal Pleistocene and that the introduction of blade technology is probably a result of these foraging groups from the north (e.g. Siberia) moving southward into the Korean Peninsula. In turn, using results derived from genetics studies, it was argued that foraging groups from southern China that still used Early Paleolithic core and flake tools also migrated northward to the Korean Peninsula (KD Bae 2010). According to KD Bae (2010), these migrations, occurring from the north and south, best explains why during the Korean Late Paleolithic we see core and flake assemblages alongside blade and microblade collections. There are two points here that somewhat complicate this model: 1) genetics studies; and 2) paleobathymetric variation.

Substantial debate exists among geneticists over the nature of modern human migration patterns in eastern Asia (as reviewed recently by Stoneking and Delfin 2010; Di and Sanchez-Mazas 2011, and noted by Norton and Jin 2009). Briefly, based on analyses of Y-chromosome haplotypes, two "Asian-specific" Y-chromosome haplogroups (O3-M122, D-M174), mtDNA and autosomal SNPs, some genetics laboratories concluded that not only did modern humans initially arrive in southern China, but there was at least one major migration northward around 30,000-25,000 BP and possibly a second one around 60,000 BP (Su et al. 1999; Yao et al. 2002; Shi et al. 2005, 2008; Abdulla et al. 2009). However, other genetics studies found a more heterozygous genetic profile among the northeast Asian samples than originally proposed, thus leading to suggestions that modern human migrations into eastern Asia could have reached the north first or moved initially in two directions skirting the Himalayan-Tibetan mountain range (Karafet et al. 2001; Xueet al. 2006; Zhonget al. 2010). Di and Sanchez-Mazas (2011: 81) recently concluded that "the disagreement between these different studies is mostly due to discrepant results on the amount of genetic diversity in NEAs [Northeast Asians] and SEAs [Southeast Asians]."

The primary point that can be drawn from these genetics studies related to this paper is that it is not at all clear whether modern humans reached southern China first and then migrated northward during glacial periods (MIS 4 and 2) reaching the Korean Peninsula in time to contribute to the development of the Late Paleolithic in that region. Related to this, a logical question that might be asked is why would modern human foraging groups move northward during glacial periods to face colder environmental conditions? If anything, during glacial periods there would have been a mass migration of floras and faunas southward in the face of southward expanding ice sheets rather than the reverse pattern (Norton et al. 2010b). This leads us to our second point. Paleobathymetric studies around the Korean peninsula have indicated that during major glacial periods (e.g. MIS 6 and MIS 2) sea levels dropped anywhere from 60 m to as much as 120 m (Park 1994, 2001; Minoura et al. 1997; Kim et al. 1999; Lee 2007). In an earlier study that evaluated the effect of paleobathymetric variation on human foraging strategies, Norton (2007) showed that during glacial periods (e.g. Last Glacial Maximum) much of the West Sea/Yellow Sea area separating eastern China and the Korean peninsula would have been dry and at times, a land connection would have existed between southern Korea and the Japanese archipelago. Indeed, much of the West Sea/Yellow Sea sits only about 50 m, with the rest sitting no more than 100 m, below current sea levels (Figure 10-3). This would have facilitated movements of floras and faunas throughout the region. With the warming period that came with the advent of MIS 1, sea levels rose to the point where some degree of territorial circumscription for mobile foragers

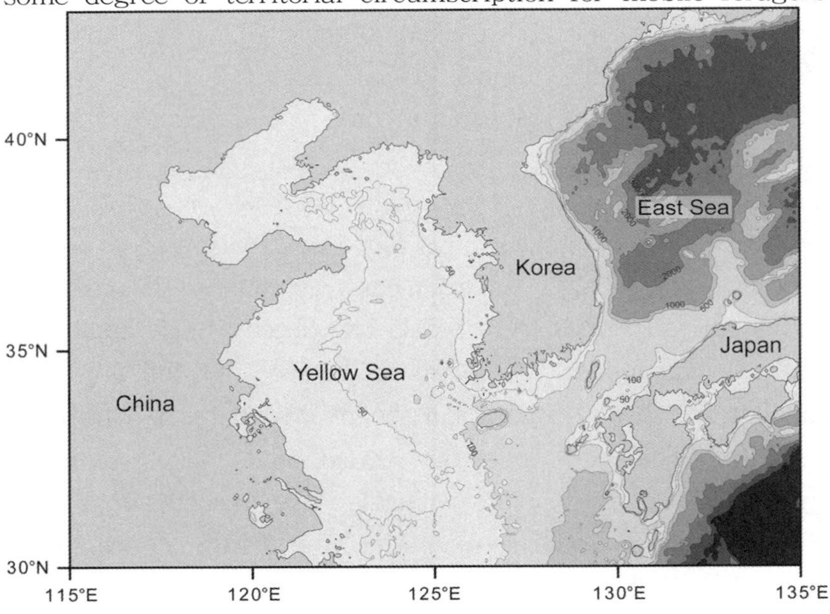

Figure 10-3. Map of the West Sea/Yellow Sea region with the estimated depths. During glacial periods a 50 m drop in sea levels would have resulted in about one half of the area as dry land. During more significant glacial periods, with more significant drops in sea levels, all of the West Sea/Yellow Sea region would have been dry land.

in the region would have occurred. Although Norton (2007) was discussing archaeological implications of hominin mobility strategies in the face of paleobathymetric variation during the Terminal Pleistocene–Middle Holocene, we suggest that these factors were equally relevant to hominin behavioral decision making and mobility strategies during MIS 3–2.

Evaluation of NGRIP data graphed for the last 130,000 years indicates that MIS 3 was a relatively warm stage, not as warm as MIS 1, but clearly warmer than MIS 4 and MIS 2 (Figure 10–4). Although sea levels around the Korean Peninsula during MIS 3 were probably not as high as today,

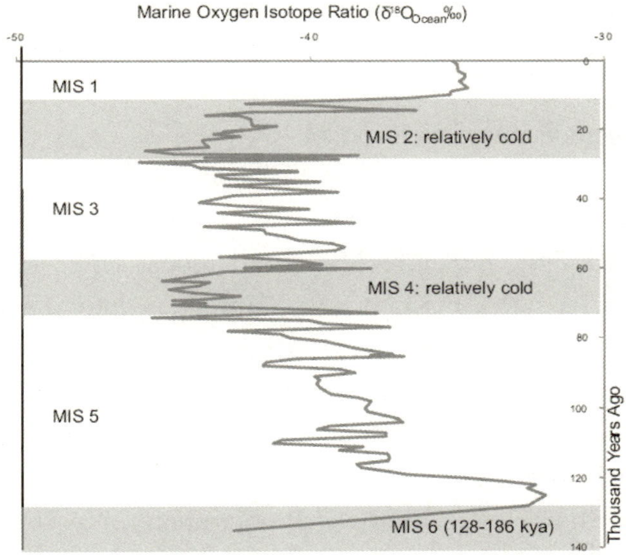

Figure 10-4. Reconstruction of the variability in marine isotope stages 1e6. Marine isotope stage data drawn from the North Greenland Ice Core Project (http://www.gfy.ku.dk/www-glac/ngrip/index_eng.htm).

they were clearly higher than during the glacial periods. This suggests that during warm stages, the West Sea/Yellow Sea would have been lower during MIS 3, but not completely dry as what probably occurred during MIS 6 and MIS 2.

In turn, this would have hindered hominin mobility strategies, particularly any that resulted in migrations northward by hominins living in southern China during MIS 3. During MIS 2, much or all of the West Sea/Yellow Sea would have been dry, which would have facilitated movement through the region. However, as we pointed out above, whywould hominin foraging groups be inclined to move northward in the face of an increasing hostile environment, particularly when many floras and faunas would have been migrating southward?

Migration/trade interaction model

This model should be viewed as a modified version of KD Bae's (2010) "North-South [Migration] Model". There are two primary differences. First, human migrations into the Korean peninsula from southern China have yet to be convincingly documented. This is despite the fact that some genetics studies suggest modern humans arrived initially in southern China and moved northward.

Any northward (or southward) migration in eastern Asia documented through genetics research need to account for factors such as varying paleobathymetry if including regions such as coastal areas and islands. In particular, in light of variability in paleobathymentry during the MIS 3-2 transition it should be fairly evident that at times hominins around the east coast of China and the Korean peninsula would have faced varying degrees of territorial circumscription. This would have included restricted direct access to the Korean peninsula from southern China during parts or most of MIS 3.

Second, if there were clear large scale migrations (resulting in presumed replacements) southward into the Korean peninsula from regions like Siberia by blade and microblade carrying human foraging groups then we might anticipate seeing breaks in the archaeological record. For instance, we might expect to see situations where Mode IV (Blades) and Mode V (Microblades) dominated stone tool technologies suddenly appear in horizons immediately overlying Mode I (Oldowan) stone toolkits. These types of cases might be interpreted as a new group of humans moving into the region. However, in Korea it is fairly well documented that between ~40,000–30,000 BP blades and tanged points begin to appear in small frequencies in strata that are still dominated by traditional Early Paleolithic core and flake stone toolkits (e.g. Yonghodong, Hwadaeri, Hopyeongdong), including sometimes bifacially worked implements (Seong 2009; KD Bae 2010). The archaeological record currently suggests that it is not until after the advent of MIS 2 that blade and microblade stone tool industries become more dominant in the Korean peninsula.

The slow introduction of blade and tanged points, rather than a quick replacement of those tool types over the Early Paleolithic stone tool industries, might actually be suggestive of some type of slow introduction of human foragers' influence into the region either through direct occasional migrations or some type of trade interactions (Norton and Jin 2009). Although it is difficult to document trade interactions during MIS 3, obsidian from sites dating to ~30,000 BP situated on the Kanto Plain in Honshu, Japan has been sourced to Kozushima (Ikawa-Smith 2008). Kozushima is an offshore island that would have been minimally separated from Honshu by at least 40 km of open water during glacial periods.

During MIS 2, there is evidence that obsidian was moved upwards of 300 ㎞ from Hokkaido to Sakhalin as early as 23,000 BP (Kuzmin et al., 2002). Arca shells appear in the Zhoukoudian Upper Cave assemblage that probably originated from the West Sea/Yellow Sea, indicating movement of at least 150 km to possibly as far away as 500-600 ㎞ depending on which date one uses for the cultural layers and where the paleocoast line would lie (Norton and Gao 2008b; Norton and Jin 2009). Although movement of obsidian and Arca shells could represent long distance migrations by mobile human foraging groups, it is possible that they also represent trade interactions (Norton and Jin 2009).

Conclusion

One point that should be clear from this synthesis is that if modern humans swept into eastern Asia carrying with them a superior stone tool industry and replacing the indigenous peoples, they do not appear to have done much sweeping in the

Korean peninsula. Indeed, we see only a few blades and tanged points in the early Late Paleolithic sites, lithic assemblages that are still dominated by the core and flake tools that represent the eastern Asian Early Paleolithic. It is only after ~30,000 BP that blades, tanged points, and microblades begin to represent a larger proportion of the overall stone tool industries. Thus, a sudden overall replacement of Early Paleolithic core and flake tool industries by blade and microblade stone toolkits is not evident in Korea. This archaeological pattern could be interpreted as evidence of a slow in situ evolutionary behavioral development (Seong 2006, 2009). However, a more parsimonious explanation is that the slow transition from core and flake tools to a heavier reliance on blades, tanged points, and eventually microblades by the end of MIS 3 is that human foraging groups physically moved down from the north (e.g. Siberia, Mongolia) in small scale migrations or these more northerly groups may have traded with indigenous peoples living in Korea during MIS 3-e2 (see also KD Bae 2010). Although it may be possible that there were large scale migrations from southern China, as we noted above, different genetics laboratories have come to very different conclusions regarding these supposed mass migrations. Including discussion of the variability of the paleobathymetry of the West Sea/Yellow Sea region during glacial and non-glacial periods further complicates arguments of mass migrations from the south into the Korean peninsula.

It is unfortunate that we cannot access the North Korean hominin fossils that date to MIS 3-2. It would be useful to conduct a detailed morphometric study of the hominin fossils from Ryonggok and Mandalli (and possibly Heungsu Child if it does indeed date to the Late Pleistocene rather than the Terminal Pleistocene or Holocene). However, a recent analysis of the Tianyuandong human fossil that dates to ~40,000 BP found some interesting similarities with western European early modern humans (Shang et al. 2007). This might support the argument of some modern human foraging groups that originated in the western Old World moving into the region after 40,000 BP and bringing with them blade technologies (Norton and Jin 2009).

Because of large scale paleoanthropological field initiatives currently being conducted in South Korea, it should only be a matter of time before good sites with adequate Pleistocene hominin and other vertebrate fossils and Paleolithic archaeology are identified (CJ Bae and KD Bae n.d.). These new sites should help clarify the nature of the Early to Late Paleolithic transition in Korea and from a broader regional perspective, eastern Asia.

CHAPTER 11

A review of Korean Microlithic Industries

Introduction

Although Palaeolithic artifacts were initially discovered at the open-air site of Dongkwanjin in the northeastern region of the Korean Peninsula in 935, the presence of microliths in Korea was only firmly established with their discovery at Kulpori (North Korea) in 1963-1964 and Sokchangni (South Korea) in 1964. Since the 1980s microliths have been recovered from excavations and surveys from at least 17 sites, the majority in South Korea. In this review, the primary Korean microlithic assemblages are discussed, along with the topics of chronology, raw material usage, and artifact typology and technology. Finally, the Korean microliths are evaluated in terms of their position in the broader Northeast Asian picture.

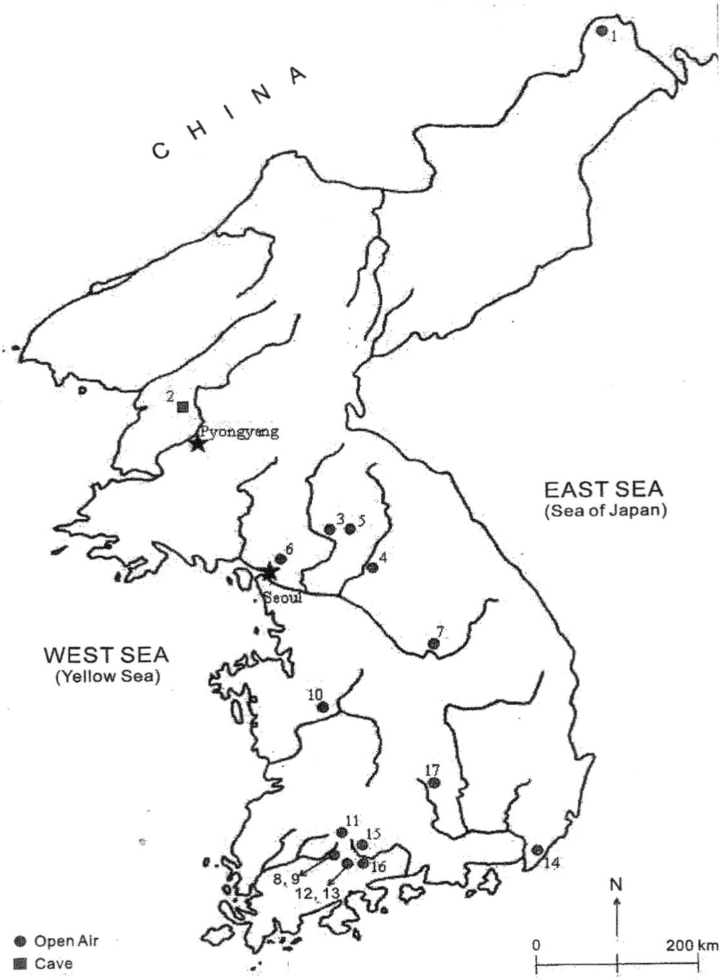

Figure 11-1. Primary microlithic yielding localities on the Korean Peninsula

1. Kulpori; 2. Mandalli; 3. Sangmuryongni; 4. Hahwagyeri; 5. Jangheungni; 6. Millakdong; 7. Suyanggae; 8. Noeundong; 9. Hwasun; 10. Sokchangni; 11. Okkwa; 12. Wolpyeong; 13. Kokcheon; 14/ Jungdong and Jwadong; 15. Kumpyung; 16. Juksan; 17. Imbilli.

Primary Microlithic Assemblages

To date, microliths have been discovered in at least 17 site in Korea (Figure 11-1). What follows is a brief description of the primary sites from the northen, central, and southern region of the Korean Peninsula. Discussion of recent developments in palaeoanthropological studies in modern day North Korea is difficult given the current state of that country`s economic and political situation. The severe economic conditions, in addition to a general 'closed door' policy, has resulted in a significant decrease in the number of detailed studies carried out in and disseminated from North Korea in the past two decades. A accordingly, it is extremely difficult for a non-North Korean scholar to estimate how many palaeoanthropological research projects are currently begin undertaken or have been carried out over the course of the past decade or so. Fortunately, due to the popularity of archaeology and an economy that is capable of supporting such social scientific research in South Korea, many archaeological surveys and excavations have been carried out south of the Demilitarized Zone (at the 38th parallel separating North and South Korea), particularly over the course of the past two decades. As a result of this interest there has been a significant increase in our overall knowledge of microlithic studies in South Korea (Chang 2002; Norton 2000).

Northern Korean Peninsula

Mandalli is a cave site located 20 ㎞ east of Pyongyang, the present day capital city of North Korea. Three stratigraphic levels were determined during excavations, with the most recent one containing excavations, with the most recent one containing excavations, with the most recent one containing Neolithic pottery sherds and bone tools. Mandalli is one of the few Palaeolithic sites on the Korean Peninsula discovered to date that has revealed Upper Palaeolithic artifacts in the same context as Homo sapiens remains as well as a large palaeontological assemblage. These Pleistocene deposits were discovered in the middle stratigraphic level. The Homo sapiens accumulation comprises a calvaria, a mandible, and fragments of another mandible, humerus, femur, and innominate. In addition, the associated faunal assemblage consists of extant animal species, including *Vulpes vulpes, Sus sp.*, and *Cervus nippon, and the extinct Hyaena sp.* Thirteen artifacts were recovered during excavations, of which seven were classified as microblade cores. Obsidian was the primary raw material utilized to produce these artifacts. Two pieces of deer antler appear to have been worked as well. In the lowest stratigraphic level only a palaeontological assemblage was recovered during excavations. Even though Mandalli lacks absolute dates, the presence of miciroblade artifacts in association with modern humans directly underlying Neolithic deposits suggests an Upper Pleistocene-Holocene period of human occupation. The presence of the cave was probably not continuous even at this late stage of cultural development (Kim et al. 1990; Norton

2000; Park 1992; Seo 1990).

Central Korean Penisula

In 1964 Sokchangni had the distinction of being the first Palaeolithic site discovered and excavated in South Korea. Between 1964 and 1992 it was excavated 12 times revealing Lower Paleolithic, Upper Palaeolithic, and Mesolothic residues. The Lower Palaeolithic deposits include choppers, chopping tools, cores, and unifacial flakes produced on local quartz and quartzite river cobbles. The Upper Palaeolithic industry is comprised of flakes and blades manufactured on non-local high quality obsidian, quartz crystal, and rhyolite. Evidence of three habitation sites with hearths may also have been discovered in the Upper Palaeolithic stratigraphic level. Two ^{14}C dates exist for the Upper Pleistocene deposits (c. 20,830 and c. 30,690 BP). Further support for an Upper Palaeolithic occupation between c. 20,000 BP and c. 17,000 BP is the presence of vertical soil cracks that Korean geologists have traditionally used as representative evidence of the last Glacial Maximum (LGM) on the Korean Peninsula. In a level situated above the Upper Palaeolithic deposits, microcores, microblades, microburins, and thumbnail scrapers were discovered. It has been difficult to obtain solid ^{14}C dates from this level due to disturbance by farmers over the course of the past five centuries, though it is believed to date to the terminal Pleistocen/Holocene transitional period (Lee and Kim 1992;

Sohn 1993).

Suyanggae is an open-air Upper Palaeolithic site located about 100 ㎞ southeast of Seoul, along the upper South Han River in Chungbuk Province. It was excavated between 1983 and 1985 by Chungbuk National University as part of a salvage archaeology project preceding construction of the Cheongju Dam. The presence of anvils, used cores, 18 refitted flaked, and debitage, in addition to a concentration of 48 tanged points suggested to the excavators that Suyanggae represents a multi-occupation site that often served as a lithic workshop. Five separate stratigraphic levels were distinguished, with a diversity of typical flake tools, cores, hammer stones, and anvils recovered from level 5 and a number of tanged points, microcores and microcore blades exposed directly above it in level 4). ^{14}C dates taken on associated charcoal suggests an occupation age range between c. 18,630 BP and c. 16,400 BP for level 4, which is the layer where the heaviest concentration of lithics was recovered (Lee 1984, 1985; Lee and Woo 1997; Lee and Yun 1994).

Even though most of the 195 microcores from Suyanggae were produced on local siliceous shale (86%), a few were made on non-local obsidian (7%), and porphyry and chert (6.4%). The interesting aspect of the obsidian utilized for the production of microblade at Suyanggae was that neutron activation analysis of the microblade cores indicated three separate sources for the obsidian. This suggests a number of interesting possible scenarios, including a hunter-gatherer group that traveled widely in search of obsidian, traded with other groups, or that different nomadic tribes occupied Suyanggae possibly at different times of even at the same time (Lee 1984, 1985; Lee and Woo 1997; Lee and Yun 1994).

The open-air site of Hahwagyeri is located along the Hongchon River in Kangwon Province. It was excavated in 1990 and 1991 by Kangwon National University Museum. Hahwagyeri is located in an ecotone where several streams meet rolling hills and with mountains as a close backdrop. This would have been an ideal location for hunter-gatherer groups to successfully hunt and fish and thus would have facilitated long-term occupation of the site. As a result of the excavations, 2,609 lithic artifacts were recovered including 21 barbs, 36 arrowheads, 27 microblade cores, and 514 microblades. The density and wide diversity of stone tools and debitage found at Hahwagyeri suggested to the excavators that this was a longterm encampment where flint-knapping took place regularly, which is additional support for the ecotone hypothesis. The microblades were primarily produced on obsidian, crystal, and quartz. It has been suggested that the obsidian used to produce the stone implements at Hahwagyeri originated from Baekdu, the highest mountain on the Korean Peninsula, though sourcing studies have yet to be conducted (Choi 1992, 1994).

Southern Korean Peninsula

A number of detailed archaeological survey carried out in the southwestern region of the Korean Peninsula over the past 15 years have revealed 27 Palaeolithic open-air sites, with the heaviest concentration of localities in the Bosung River basin. The largest and most extensively studied locality found in this region is Wolpyeong. Excavations conducted in 1998 and 2001 by Chosun University revealed cultural deposits within a 66,000 ㎡ area. Eight separate stratigraphic levels were identified with the heaviest concentration of artifacts in layers 4 (9,465 specimens) and 3 (1,300 specimens). Among the lithics, 30 conjoinable flakes and cores were discovered. These characteristics at Wolpyeong suggest that this was a place that served as a home base for extended stays and/or was visited fairly frequently. Blades, microblades, microblade cores were made primarily of rhyolite, while the rest of the stone tools were produced in vein quartz, with a smaller percentage made of tuff and rhyoite. Vein quartz was available locally, while rhyolite and tuff sources are located roughly 10 ㎞ away. Based on comparative studies with lithic assemblages from other sites (e.g. Suyanggae) and reologic reconstruction, it is thought that Wolpyeong was occupied between c. 14,000 BP and c. 12,000 BP (Lee 1997, 2002a, 2002b)

Chronology

Chronological reconstruction of Palaeolothic sites in Korea have traditionally been problematic. For instance, the age of occupation of the Lower Palaeolithic site of Chongokni has led to a spirited debate with dates ranging between 350,000 years ago and c. 30,000 BP (Bae 2002; Danhara et al. 2002, Norton 2000; Norton et al. 2004; Seong 2004a; Yi 199, 1996; Yi et al. 1998). One of the primary reasons of the difficulty of obtaining absolute dates in Korean archaeological studies is that the acidic soil prohibits preservation of biodegradable materials at just about all open-air sites that date to the Pleistocene, resulting in a paucity of reliable 14C dates for Palaeolithic sites. Currently, the earliest dated microlithics on the Korean Peninsula are from the Jangheungni site in central Korea with a ^{14}C date of 24,200 ± 600 BP (but see Seong, this volume). Sokchangni and Suyangae have 14C dates that range between c. 20,000 BP and c. 16,000 BP indicating that microlithic technology was more prevalent at the beginning of the LGM (Chang 2002; Lee and Woo 1998; Lee and Yun 1994).

Instead of utilizing radiocarbon dating, Korean aechaeologists have often had to rely on other markers in order to build a general chronological sequence for the transition from blade to microblade technology. For instance, determining presence/absence of AT (Aira-Tanzawa) tephra at archeological sites in Korea has become more common over the past decade. The AT tephra originates from a volcanic explosion of the Aira caldera that occurred at c. 24,000 BP in Kyushu (Japan), and its presence at archaeological sites as far north as Chongokni and the Shandong Peninsula in northeastern China indicates the extent of the explosion itself (Figure 11-2). The presence of AT tephra is often used to date many of the Upper Palaeolithic sites in Korea (for example, Koraeri

Miryang), though it has sometimes been employed to support chronological reconstructions of Lower Palaeolithic sites as well (such as Chongokni). Even though the AT tephra predates most microlithic sites in Korea, its presence contributes to the reconstruction of chronological sequences of the tran-

Figure 11-2. AT tephra shown by lines (after Eden et al. 1996)

sition from blade to microblade technologies (Imamura 1996; Norton 2000; Norton et al. 2004; Seong 1998; Yi et al. 1998).

Another useful marker is the presence of vertical soil cracks in stratigraphic profile (see above). Although there is no conclusive evidence for the formation of these cracks it is believed that they form during cold climates (further studies in Alaska appear to support this hypotheses). Accordingly, the presence of these 'ice wedges' is often thought represent a chronological period around the LGM. Many of the microcores from the Korean Peninsula are found in stratigraphic levels that either contain these ice wedges or are located directly above them (Lee and Kim 1992; Yi 1989).

In many cases, site chronologies have been based in lithic typologies. For instance, microcores from Suyanggae, Kokcheon, Tanjon, and the lower layer of Sokchangni are characterized as being wedge-shaped with long, single striking platforms. These are considered to be the oldest type of microcore present on the Korean Peninsula. The younger group of microcores display a general decrease in size, a greater diversity in raw material utilized, a simplification of technological processes, evidence of multiple striking platforms on individual cores, and the presence of more exhausted cores. Representative microlithic assemblages are from Wolpyeing, Sanmuryongni, Jungdong, Hahwagyeri, and the upper layer of Sokchangni (Chang 2002).

It is still not well established when microlothic industries disappear from the Korean Peninsula. In general, a diversity of small quartz tools, in addition to pottery sherds and ground stone tools, appear in stratigraphic deposits above microlithic tools. Examples of this are found at Hahwagyeri and Sokchangni. Probably the most representative site of this transition is Kosanni, located on Jeju Island off the southern coast of Korea and dating presumably to c. 10,400–10,200 BP. During the excavations at Kosanni 470 microblades were found in association with 700 projectile points, scrapers, bifaces, burins, and over 1,900 Chulmun pottery sherds. This combination of tool types in direct association with pottery is representative of the Upper Palaeolithic/Incipicent Neolithic transition in Korea (CNUM 1998; Choi 1994; Norton 2007;

Park 1992).

Raw Materials

One possible explanation for the origin of blade and micro-blade technology in Korea is based on the quality of raw material. It is generally accepted that quartz and quartzite stone tools normally comprise 90-95% of palaeolithic assemblages in Korea. However, quartz and quartzite are difficult raw materials to work, particularly in the production of uniform tools (Kuhn 1995; Whittaker 1994). With the increased need to produce more standardized stone implements through time it has been suggested that higher quality raw materials were utilized (e.g. obsidian, shale, and tuff), often deriving from non-local sources (Chang 2002; Seong 1998, 2004a). The increased utilization of different raw materials appears to coincide with the transition from the Lower to Upper Palaeolithic in Korea, similar to what occurred in China (Gao and Norton 2002). As evidence from other regions of Northeast Asia (for example, Mongolia: Brantingham et al. 2000) suggests, however, raw material constrains cannot completely explain the increased diversity that is associated with the Lower to Upper Palaeolithic transition as it is clear that knappers were capable of getting the most out of the local quartz and quartzite river cobbles in Korea, for example, at the Hahwagyeri site.

Regional diversity in raw material utilized in the production of microcores is present in Korea and can be divided into toe northern, central, and southern regions. In the north, obsidian believed to have originated fro, the Baekdu Mountain source was the raw material of choice for microcores and microblade production during the terminal Pleistocene (for example, at the Mandalli site). In the central region of the Korean Peninsula, siliceous shale is the most common raw material utilized as evidence from the Suyanggae and Sokchangni lithic assemblages indicates. In the southern region of Korea, microcores were produced on volcanic tuff, with some also produced on siltstone, hornfels, andesite, and obsidian (e.g. at the Wolpyeong, Taejon, and Okkwa sites) (Lee 2002a; Seong 1998; Yi et al. 1990a). It may be possible that the obsidian found in the southern region originated from the Baekdu Mountain source in the north. However, the more parsimonious explanation for the presence of obsidian found in the southern region originated from the Baekdu Mountain source in the north. However, the more parsimonious explanation for the presence of obsidian in the southern region of Korea is that it originated from sources on Kyushu Island in Japan. Only sourcing studies will help to clarify this question.

Typology and Technology

Typological reconstructions of the Korean microcore industries are generally based on the condition of the striking platform, location of microflaking, blank types, and blank preparation. The majority of the Korean microcores belong to the wedge-shaped core category. However, some microcores have been characterized as being conical instead. It is believed that the conical-shaped cores are simply more exhausted forms of wedge-shaped cores. In addition to microcores and microblades, Korean microlithic assemblages are generally comprised of burins, side scrapers, end scrapers, borers, and tanged points, the later tool type similar to that found in penecotemporaneous Japan (Chang 2002; Lee 2002a; Matsufuji 1987, 1997; Seong 1998).

For typological studies of Koran microlithic industies perhaps the most significant site is Suyanggae. This site is important nor only due to the large number of microcores and microblades that were excavated in situ, but also because the first attempts of typological and technological analyses of Korean microlithic industries were conducted on the associated artifacts. The Suyanggae microcores can be classified into three types based in the morpholgy of the striking platform, plain context, and flake scar direction. Type I produced microblades that were semi-lunate or boat-shaped through pressure flaking on unprepared platforms. Type II cores had platforms prepared by longitudinal flaking, followed by pressure flaking on the resulting microblades. Type III cores had platforms prepared initially by latitudinal pressure flaking (Lee and Woo 1998; Lee and Yun 1994). These microblade manufacturing techniques are similar to the Yubetsu method in Japan (Aikens and Higuchi 1982), and the Hetao and Sanggan techniques in China (Chen 1984; Gai 1985).

Preliminary comparative studies have been conducted on the

Suyanggae (central Korea) and Wolpyeong (southern Korea) micricore assemblages. It has been suggested that variation exists on the striking platforms of the microcores from the two sites. In particular, analyses have indicated that on further retouch was conducted on the Suyanggae microcores once the spall was detached for the modification of the striking platform. In the case of the microcores form the Wolpyeng site, it is believed that additional retouch was carried out which served to further flatten the striking platform. The inter-assemblage variation could be the result of a number of different developments: 1) to some extent different stages of the reduction process; 2) variation in raw materials (Suyanggae: siliceous shale; Wolpyeong: rhyolite and tuff); and/or 3) different functions employed by hunter-gatherers. The additional retouching on the Wolpyeong microcores has led to suggestions that Suyanggae is the older one of the two sites. Also suggestive is that Suyanggae has a 14C date range of c. 18,000–16,000 BP, while artifacts from Wolpyeong have many similarities with the stone toolkit from the Shiraraki Hattoridai site in Japan with a 14C date of c. 14,000 BP (Chang 2002; Lee 2002a).

Origin and Dispersal of Korean Microlithic Technology

East Asian microlithic technology is most noted for the presence of wedge-shaped cores that initially appeared in northern

China between c. 50,000 years ago and c. 28,000 BP. Korean microlithics are considered as on branch of the general East Asian tradition developing sometime after this period. It is relatively easy to build a case for the origin of microlithic technology on the Korean Peninsula to have veen a direct result of diffusion from China with some of the technology eventually moving to the Japanese Archipelago through bilateral relations with hunter-gatherer groups from that region. It is not as easy to develop a rationale for the indigenous development of microlithic technology in Korea. Let us first examine the case for diffusion of microlithic knapping technology from China and interaction with hunter-gatherers from Japan.

Up to the early 1970s it was generally believed in China that microliths were only associated with Neolithic and Bronze Age cultural periods. It was not until 1972 that the development of microlithic industries could be pushed back to at least the Upper Palaeolithic. Microcores first began to appear in Chinese Upper Palaeolithic sites between c. 50,000 years ago to c. 28,000 BP. The two primary early sites for the appearance of microliths in China are Salawusu (Uranium-series dates range: c. 50,000-37,000 years ago; ^{14}C date c. 35,340 BP) and Shiyu (^{14}C date c. 28,135 BP). These early dates notwithstanding, microliths do not become common on China until the Upper Palaeolithic/Neolithic transitional stage. It is generally believed that Middle Palaeolithic complexes from Mongola and/or the Dyuktai culture from siveria influenced the development of microlithic technology in northern China (Brantingham et al. 2000; Chen 1984; Gai 1985; Gao and

Norton 2002; Yi and Clark 1985; Zhang 2000).

Jangheungni, with ^{14}C dates of around 24,000 BP, currently represents the earliest appearance of microliths in Korea, followed by Sokchangni and Suyanggae with ^{14}C dates between c. 20,00 BP and c. 16,000 BP. All of these dates postdate the appearance of miroliths at Salawusu and Shiyu in China, suggesting that microlithic technology first arose in China and then later spread to other regions of East Asia.

However, the recent discovery of tanged points in stratigraphic levels radiocarbon dated to 38,500±1000 BP(SNU00-261)(Bae and Kim 2003) at the Yonghodong site in central Korea indicates that more advanced lithic technology could have arrived on the Korean Peninsula earlier than generally accepted (Han 2002). Tanged points and microcores are sometimes found in the same stratigraphic levels in Korea [for instance, at Suyanggae (Lee 1984, 1985; Lee and Woo 1998; Lee and Yun 1994)]. Only additional research at the Yonghodong site will reveal whether the ^{14}C date is reliable of the stratigraphic units with two tanged points were subjected to some degree of mixing of younger and older deposits. In addition, microliths have not been found in the same context as the tanged points at Yonghodong. However, if further studies support the Yonghodong findings it could be used as evidence for at least a semi-indigenous development of microlithic technology on the Korean Peninsula that is penecontemporaneous with that from China.

It is clear that microlithic technology discovered on the Korean Peninsula was very similar to what has been found in the Russian Far East around the same time. For instance, tanged points similar to those from Suyanggae are known from the open-air site of Ustinoka 1 in the eastern Primorye region of the Russian Far East, indicative of possible cultural contact. Similar backed knives and tanged points appear in archaeological deposits ait the Oita site on Kyushu as well suggesting that the technology could have either diffused through Sakhalin Island in the north of from the southern Korean Peninsula. Similar lithic techniques (e.g., Yubetsu, Horoka, and Togeshita) across a very broad region (Korea, Japan, and the Russian Far East) suggest at least minimal cultural contact. The presence of obsidian from Hokkaido in archaeological deposits in Sakhalin and obsidian in southern Korea possibly from nearby Kyushu is further evidence for cultural contact and/or hunter-gatherer migrations throughout the circum-Sea of Japan region (Aikens and Higuchi 1982; Imamura 1996; Kononenko 1997; Kuzmin 2002; Kuzmin et al. 2002; Matsufuji 1987, 1997).

Conclusion : Future Directions

Although a number of well excavated and studied sites close to 30 have been found, there are still a few limitations that hinder more comprehensive research on the origin and development of microlithic industries on the Korean Peninsula. For instance, probably the most significant problem with the current state of Korean microlithic studies is the dearth of known research in North Korea. Still the two best-known microlithic sites in North Korea are Kulpori and Mandalli, but these were discovered and excavated over a quarter of a century ago. Hopefully, in the future with change in the political and economic environment on the Korean Peninsula, more collabratove research that involves North Korean scholars will facilitate research geared toward reconstructing the origin and development of microlithic technology across the entire Korean Peninsula.

Three other factors would greatly strengthen the quality of microlithic research in Korea Palaeolothic studies. Firstly, obtaining more absolute dates is critical to reconstructing Upper Palaeolithic life ways. Due to the paucity of radiocarbon dates it is difficult to develop concrete chronological sequences for site occupation on the Korean Peninsula during the terminal Pleistocene and into the Early Holocene. Secondly, more detailed raw material sourcing analyses are needed to reconstruct general hunter-gatherer mobility patterns and levels of interactions, similar to what has been done in investigating Upper Palaeolithic-Early Neolithic hunter-gatherer movement between Sakhalin and Hokkaido (Kuzmin et al. 2002). Thirdly, a paucity of associated fanual remains from Korean sites has resulted in a lack of attempts at reconstructing subsistence patterns of Upper Palaeolithic hunter-gatherers. We are currently planning research specifically designed to address many of these questions.

In the future more advanced typological and technological reconstructions will be conducted on the Korean materials. In addition, with increased studies of these microlithic sites, a stronger chronological model will be developed. It is believed that more detailed analysis of mircoliths from recently excavated sites (e.g. Wolpyeong) should reveal information regarding the reduction sequences of the microcores. Future research on Korean microlithic industries will lead to a more comprehensive synthesis of hunter-gatherer life ways and their interaction with other groups in Northeast Asia.

References

Abdulla, M.A., Ahmed, I., Assawamakin, A., Bhak, J., Brahmachari, S.K., Calacal, G.C., Chaurasia, A., Chen, C.H., Chen, J., Chen, Y.T., et al., 2009. Mapping human genetic diversity in Asia. Science 326, pp. 1541-1545.

Aigner, J.S., 1981. Archaeological Remains in Pleistocene China. Verlag C.H. Beck, Munchen, Germany.

Asfaw, B., Beyne, Y., Suwa, G., Walter, R.C., White, T.D., WoldeGabriel, G., Yemane, T., 1992. The earliest Acheulean from Konso-Gardula. Nature 360, pp. 732-735.

Bae, C.J., 2010. The late Middle Pleistocene hominin fossil record of eastern Asia: synthesis and review. Yearbook of Physical Anthropology 53, pp. 75-93.

Bae, C.J., Kim, J.C., 2010. The Late Paleolithic-Neolithic transition in Korea: current archaeological and radiocarbon perspectives. Radiocarbon 52, pp. 493-499.

Bae, K.D., 1988. The Significance of the Chongokni Stone Industry in the Tradition of Paleolithic Culture in East Asia. Ph.D. Dissertation, University of California, Berkeley.

Bae, K.D., 1989. The development of the Hantan River Basin, Korea and the age of the sediment on the top of the Chongok Basalt. Korean Journal of Quaternary Research 3, pp. 87-101.

Bae, K.D., 1992. Preliminary report of the Kumpari Paleolithic site, Paju, central Korea. Seoul. J. Kor. Stud. 5, pp. 127-140.

Bae, K.D., 1994. Paleolithic tradition of East Asia: Chongoknian, presence of few bifaces in Paleolithic stone industries, Paleolithic Culture of East Asia. National Research Institute of Cultural Properties. Seoul, pp. 193-211.

Bae, K.D., 1997. A study of stone industries of Korea. Korean J.

Quatern. Res.
Bae, K.D., 1998. Formation processes of depressions of the Kumpari Paleolithic site, Paju, central Korea. Korean J. Quatern. Res. 12, pp. 45–53 (in Korean).
Bae, K.D., 2000a. Comparative archaeology in prehistoric culture in East Asia and East Africa. J. Korean Archaeol. Soc. 43, pp. 1–39 (in Korean).
Bae, K.D., 2000b. Transformation processes of Paleolithic sites in Korea, Journal of Korean Paleolithic Archaeology Society 1, pp. 45–56.
Bae, K.D., 2001. Lower and Middle Paleolithic Industries in the Korean Peninsula, Paleolithic Archaeology 62. pp. 1–10 (in Japanese).
Bae, K.D., 2002a. Chongokni Paleolithic site: current understandings. In: Bae, K.D., Lee, J.C. (Eds.), Paleolithic Archaeology in Northeast Asia. Yeoncheon County and The Institute of Cultural Properties, Seoul & Yeoncheon County, pp. 55–75.
Bae, K.D., 2002b. Radiocarbon dates from Paleolithic sites in Korea. Radiocarbon 44, pp. 473–476.
Bae, K.D., 2003a. Origin and development of Upper Paleolithic industries in the Korean peninsula. Korean Journal of Quaternary Research 17 (2), pp. 101–103.
Bae, K.D., 2003b. Review of Chronological Researches of the Chongokni site, In: (K. D. Bae & J. C. Lee, Eds.) Paleolithic Archaeology in Northeast Asia. Yeoncheon County, Korea: Yeoncheon County & The Institute of Cultural Properties Seoul, pp. 13–20.
Bae, K.D., 2007. Stone Industry of the Mansuri site and Provision of Korean Paleolithic Research. In Proceedings of Prehistoric Seminar of the Mansuri Paleolithic Site, Cheongwon, pp. 47–58.
Bae, K.D., 2008. Results and Perspective of the Chongokni Paleolithic Studies. In: Basic Studies of the Paleolithic Chronology and Paleoenvironmental Changes in East Asia. Kyoto, pp. 113–122.
Bae, K.D., 2010. Origin and patterns of the Upper Paleolithic industries

in the Korean Peninsula and movement of modern humans in East Asia. Quaternary International 211 (1-2), pp. 103-112.

Bae, K.D., Chung, H.J., Kim, D.I., Kim, Y.Y., Chun, B.H., Lee, J.C., Lee, C.M., 2004. Archaeological and Ethnoarchaeological Research of Early Prehistoric Culture in Tanzania. Institute of Cultural Properties, Hanyang University, Seoul (in Korean).

Bae, K.D., Hwang, S.H., Im, D.I., 1999. The Kumpari Paleolithic Site Report of Excavation in 1989-1992. National Research Institute of Cultural Properties, Seoul (in Korean).

Bae, K.D., H.Y. Lee and K.R. Kim. 2006. Report of excavation of the locality 4, Mansuri, Chongwon, Hankukgogohak (Korean Archaeology) 4, pp. 92-107.

Bae, K.D., Hong, M.Y., Lee, H.Y., Kim, Y.Y., 2001. The Chongokni Paleolithic Site Report of Test Pit Excavation, 2000-2001. Yeoncheon County and Institute of Cultural Properties. Hanyang University, Ansan.

Bae, K.D., Kim, J.C., 2003. Radiocarbon chronology of the Palaeolithic complexes and the transition to the Neolithic in Korea. The Review of Archaeology 24, pp. 46-49.

Bae, K.D., Lee, H.Y., Shin, Y.H., Hwang, S.H., Oh, Y.S., 1995. Report of Excavation of the Chongokni Paleolithic Site 1994-95. Hanyang Anthropological Series, vol. 6, Hanyang University, Seoul (in Korean).

Binford, L.R., 1981. Bones: Ancient Men and Modern Myth. Academic Press, New York.

Binford, L.R., 1984. Faunal Remains from Klasies River Mouth. Academic Press, New York.

Blumenschine, R.J., 1995. Percussion marks, tooth marks, and experimental determination of the timing of hominid and carnivore access to long bones at FLK Zinjanthropus, Olduvai Gorge, Tanzania. Journal of Human Evolution 29, pp. 21-51.

Blumenschine, R.J., Marean, C.W., 1993. A carnivore's view of archaeological bone assemblages. In: Hudson, J. (Ed.), From Bones to Behavior. Center for Archaeological Investigations, Carbondale, IL, pp. 273-301.

Blumenschine, R.J., Pobiner, B.L., 2006. Zooarchaeology and the ecology of Oldowan hominin carnivory. In: Ungar, P.S. (Ed.), Evolution of the Human Diet. Oxford University Press, Oxford, pp. 167-190.

Brantingham, P.J., Kuhn, S.L., 2001. Constraints on Levallois core technology: a mathematical model. Journal of Archaeological Science 28 (7), 747-761.

Chang, W.J., 1989. Origin of Korean People (Josunsaram uy Giwon). Social Science Press. Pyoungyang.

Chang, W.J., 1990.Several Anthropological Problems of the Ryokpo Man, Chosungogoyonku (Study of Chosun Archaeology) 74, pp. 22-27.

Chang, W.J., 2002. Origin of Korean People. Baekkasajeonchulpansa, Pyongyang.

Choi, B.K., 2007. A study on the Hwadae-ri Shimteo Paleolithic site in Pocheon-city, the Korean peninsula. Journal of the Korean Paleolithic Society 15, pp. 57-68.

Choi, B.K., Choi, S.Y., Lee, H.Y., Cha, J.H., 2001. Jangheungni (Janghung-ri) Paleolithic Site. Institute of Archaeology, Kangwon University, Chuncheon.

Choi, B.K., Ryu, H.J., 2005. The Hwadae-ri Shimteo Paleolithic Site, Pocheon. Kangwon National University, Chuncheon, Korea.

Choi, M.J., 1994. Report of second excavation at Namkaeri Paleolithic Site. In: Jang, K.H. (Ed.), BosungeHantan River Basin Paleolithic Sites. National Research Institute of Cultural Properties, Seoul, pp. 63-234 (in Korean).

Chung, Y.H., 1978. New find of Acheulean Hanaxe Bifaces at the Chongokni site, Youngdaemunhwa 11, pp.5-34.

Clark, J.D., 1994. The Acheulean Industrial Complex in Africa and elsewhere. In: Corruccini, R.S., Ciochon, R.L. (Eds.), Integrative Paths to the Past: Paleoanthropological Advances in Honor of F. Clark Howell. Prentice-Hall, Englewood Cliffs, NJ, pp. 451-469.

Clark, J.D., Schick, K.D., 1988. Context and content: impressions of Palaeolithic sites and assemblages in the People's Republic of China. J. Hum. Evol. 17, pp. 439-448.

Clark, J.D.,1982.Reporton the visit to palaeolithic sites in korea. Munhwajae 15 pp. ,134-140.

Corvinus, G., 2004. Homo erectus in East and Southeast Asia, and the questions of the age of the species and its association with stone artifacts, with special attention to handaxe-like tools. Quaternary International. 117, pp. 141-151.

Danhara, T., 2007. Report of Tephra Analysis of the Mansuri site in Korea (unpublished).

Danhara, T., Bae, K.D., Okada, T., Matsufuji, K., Hwang, S.H., 2002. What is the real age of the Chongokni Paleolithic site? In: Bae, K.D., Lee, J.C. (Eds.), Paleolithic Archaeology in Northeast Asia. Yeoncheon County & The Institute of Cultural Properties, Seoul & Yeoncheon County, pp. 77-116.

Danhara, T., 2008. Volcanic Glasses Found in the Sediments of Paleolithic Site in Korean and China, and their Comparison with Widespread Tephras. In: Basic Studies of the Paleolithic Chronology and Paleoenvironmental Changes in East Asia. Kyoto, pp. 41-51

Derevianko, A.P., 2005a. The earliest human migration in Eurasia and the origin of the Upper Paleolithic. In: Derevianko, A.P. (Ed.), The Middle to Upper Paleolithic Transition in Eurasia, Hypothesis and Facts. Institute of Archaeology and Ethnography Press, Novosibirsk, pp. 5-19.

Derevianko, A.P., 2005b. The Middle to Upper Paleolithic transition in the Altai (Mongolia and Siberia). In: Derevianko, A.P. (Ed.), The Middle to Upper Paleolithic Transition in Eurasia, Hypothesis and Facts. Institute of Archaeology and Ethnography Press, Novosibirsk,

pp. 183-216.
Derevianko, A.P., 2008. The Paleolithic of Northern Asia: hypothesis and facts. In: Derevianko, A.P., Shunkov, M.V. (Eds.), The Current Issues of Paleolithic Studies in Asia. Proceedings of the International Symposium, Asian Paleolithic Association. Publishing Department of the Institute of Archaeology and Ethnography, Novosibirsk, pp. 34-41.
Derevianko, A.P., Shunkov, M.V., 2004. Formation of the Upper Paleolithic transition in the Altai. Archaeology, Ethnology and Anthropology of Eurasia 3 (1), pp. 12-40.
Di, D., Sanchez-Mazas, A., 2011. Challenging views on the peopling history of East Asia: the story according to HLA markers. American Journal of Physical Anthropology 145, pp. 81-96.
Foley, R., Lahr, M.M., 1997. Mode 3 technologies and the evolution of modern humans. Camb. Archaeol. J. 7, pp. 3-36.
Gai, P., 1985. Microlithic industries in China. In: Wu, R.K., Olsen, J. (Eds.), Paleoanthropology and Paleolithic Archaeology in the PRC. Academic Press, New York.
Gao, X., 1999. A discussion of the "Chinese Middle Paleolithic." Acta Anthropol. Sinica 18, pp. 1-16 (in Chinese).
Gao, X., 2000. Explanations of typological variability in Paleolithic remains from Zhoukoudian locality 15, China. Ph.D. Dissertation, University of Arizona, Tucson.
Gao, X., Norton, C.J., 2002. A critique of the Chinese 'Middle Palaeolithic'. Antiquity 76 (292), 3, pp. 97-412.
Gao, X., Pei, S.W., Wang, H.M., Zhong, K., 2004. A report on Paleolithic reconnaissance in Ningxia, north China. Acta Anthropologica Sinica 23 (4), pp. 307-325.
Gowlett, J.A.J., 1986. Culture and conceptualization e the Oldowan e Acheulean gradient. In: Bailey, G.N., Callow, P. (Eds.), Studies in Memory of Charles McBurney. Cambridge University Press, Cambridge, pp. 243-260.

Gowlett, J.A.J., Crompton, R.H., 1994. Kariandusi: Acheulean morphologyand the question of allometry. Afr. Archaeol. Rev. 12, 1-40.

Gyeongnam Development Institute, 2004. The Paleolithic Site at Jeongjang-ri. Gyeongnam Development Institute, Geochang.

Han, C.G., 2002. Yonghodong Paleolithic site at Daejeon, Korea. In: Bae, K.D., Lee, J.C. (Eds.), Paleolithic Archaeology in Northeast Asia. Yeoncheon County and the Institute of Cultural Properties. Hanyang University, pp. 163-172.

Han, C.K., 2003. Chronological problems of the Korean Paleolithic sites. Journal of the Korean Paleolithic Society 7, pp. 1-39.

Han, C.K., 2008. Natural environment of Upper Paleolithic period in Korea. Journal of Korean Archaeological Society 66, pp. 4-47.

Hayashida, A., 2006. Magnetic Properties of the Quaternary Sediments at the Chongokni Paleolithic Site: Comparison with Chinese Loess and Paleosol, Proceeding of Geological Research and New Age Dates of the Chongokni Paleolithic Site. Institute of Cultural Properties, Hanyang University, pp. 11-12.

Henshilwood, C.S., Marean, C.W., 2003. The origin of modern human behavior: critique of the models and their test implications. Current Anthropology 44 (5), 627-651.

Hong, M.Y., Kim, J.H., 2008. Hopyeong-dong Paleolithic Site. Korea Land Corporation, Gyeonggi Cultural Foundation and Gijeon Institute of Cultural Properties, Suwon.

Hong, S., Dong, Y.L., Wen, B., Xiao, C.J., Underhill, P.A., Shen, P.D., Chakraborty, R.,

Hou, Y. M., Potts, R., Yuan, B. Y., Guo, Z. T., Deino, A., Wang, W., Clark, J., Xie, G. M. & Huang, W.W. 2000. Mid-Pleistocene Acheulean-like stone technology of the Bose Basin, South China. Science 287, pp. 1622-1626.

Huang, W. W. 1989. Bifaces in China. Human Evolution 4, pp. 87-92.

Huang, W. W.,1993.Typology of the heavy-duty implements in the East and Southeast Asian Lower Paleolithic andacomment on the Movius typological system. Acta Anthropological Sinica 12, pp. 297–304 (in Chinese).

Huang, W.W., 1987. Bifaces in China. Acta Anthropol. Sinica 6, 61–68 (in Chinese).

Huang, W.W., 1989. Bifaces in China. Human Evolution. 4, pp. 87–92.

Huang, W.W., 1993. Typology of the heavy-duty implements in the East and Southeast Asian Lower Paleolithic and a comment on the Movius typological system. Acta Anthropol. Sinica 12, pp. 297–304 (in Chinese).

Ikawa-Smith, F., 1978. Introduction. In: Ikawa-Smith, F. (Ed.), Early Paleolithic in South and East Asia. Mouton, The Hague, pp. 1–10.

Ikawa-Smith, F., 2008. Living on the edge of the continent: the Japanese archipelago 30,000e8,000 cal. B.C. North Pacific Prehistory 2, pp. 45–64.

Isaac, G.L., 1977. Olorgesailie: Archaeological Studies of a Middle Pleistocene Lake Basin in Kenya. University of Chicago Press, Chicago.

Isaac, G.L., 1984. The archaeology of human origins: studies of the Lower Pleistocene in East Africa 1971e1981. Adv. World Archaeology. 3, pp. 1–87.

Izuho, M., Sato, H., 2008. Landscape evolution and cultural changes in the Upper Paleolithic of northern Japan. In: Derevianko, A.P., Shunkov, M.V. (Eds.), The Current Issues of Paleolithic Studies in Asia. Proceeding of the International Symposium, Asian Paleolithic Association. Publishing Department of the Institute of Archaeology and Ethnography, Novosibirsk, pp. 69–77.

Jang, Y.J., 2001. The Study of Core from Milyang Koryeri Site in Paleolithic Age. MA Thesis in the Department of Archaeology, Pusan University.

Jang, Y.J., 2007. A Study on Technique and Chronology of Upper

Paleolithic Age in Korea. Hakyon Press, Seoul.

Jeon, B.H. and N.J. Hyun., 2005. Preliminary report of the excavation of the Paleolithic localities in the Janggi Development Area, Journal of Korean Paleolithic Archaeology Society11, pp. 45–53.

Jeon, J.H., et al., 1986. Yonggok Cave Site. Science & Encyclopedia Press, Pyongyang.

Jia, L., Huang, W.W., 1985. The late Paleoltihic of China. In: Wu, R.K., Olsen, J. (Eds.), Paleoanthropology and Paleolithic Archaeology in the PRC. Academic Press, New York, pp. 211–223.

Jin, L., Su, B., 2000. Natives or immigrants: modern human origins in East Asia. Nature Review Genetics 1, pp. 126–133.

Jin, L., Ju, B., 2005. Y-chromosome evidence of southern origin of the East Asianspecific Haplogroup O3-M122. American Journal of Human Genetics 77, pp. 408–419.

Johnson, C.R., McBrearty, S., 2010. 500,000 year old blades from the Kapthurin Formation, Kenya. Journal of Human Evolution 58, pp. 193–200.

Jones, P.R., 1979. Effects of raw materials on biface manufacture. Science 204, pp. 835–836.

JRICH (Jungang Research Institute of Cultural Heritage), 2007. The Yongsan-dong Paleolithic Site. Jungang Research Institute of Cultural Heritage, Daejon, Korea.

Jun, J.H., Yoon, J., Kim, K.S., Ryu, J.K., 1986. Excavation report of Ryonggok Cave Site, Pyongyang. In: Han, C.K. (Ed.), Prehistoric Archaeology of North Korea (1990). Paeksanmunhwa, Seoul, pp. 110–114.

Karafet, T., Xu, L., Du, R., Wang, W., Feng, S., Wells, R.S., Redd, A.J., Zegura, S.L., Hammer, M.F., 2001. Paternal population history of East Asia: sources, patterns, and microevolutionary processes. American Journal of Human Genetics 69 (3).

Keates, S.G., 2000. Early andMiddle Pleistocene HominidBehaviour in

Northern China. In: British Archaeological Reports 863. Archaeopress, Oxford.

Keates, S.G., 2001. Perspectives on 'Middle Palaeolithic' settlement patterns in China. In: Conard, N.J. (Ed.), Settlement Dynamics of the Middle Paleolithic and Middle Stone Age. Kerns Verlag, Tubingen, pp. 153-175.

Keates, S.G., 2002. The Movius Line: fact or fiction? Bull. IPPA 22, pp. 17-24.

Kim, G.S., 1991. On the mammalian fauna of the Ryonggok cave 1. Kwahakwontongbo (Newsletter of Science) (Korean) 225, pp. 48-53.

Kim, J.Y. 2007. Quarternary Geology of the Mansuri site, Cheongwon. In Proceedings of Prehistoric Seminar of the Mansuri Paleolithic Site, Cheongwon, pp. 59-76.

Kim, J.Y., Lee, G.K., Yang, D.Y., Hong, S.S., Nam, U.H., Lee, J.Y., 2004. Distribution and formation of Quaternary deposits in South Korea. Journal of Korean Paleolithic Society 10, pp. 1-23.

Kim, J.Y., Lee, H.J., Yang, D.Y., 2002. Environment and chronology of Quaternary sediments of Paleolithic sites in Korea. Journal of Korean Paleolithic Society 6, pp. 165-80.

Kim, J.Y., Lee, Y.J., 2006. La stratigraphie du Pleistocene superieur et le Paleolithique en Coree Stratigraphy of the Upper Pleistocene and Paleolithic in Korea. L'anthropologie 110, pp. 119-138.

Kim, S.G., et al., 1985. Excavation Report on Sites around Pyongyang. Science & Encyclopedia Press, Pyongyang.

Kim, S.K., K.K. Kim, K.H. Baek, W.J. Chang and K.T Seo., 1985. Report of Excavation of Daehyundong cave, Ryokpoku, Excavation Report of Caves sites in Pyoungyang Area. Science Encyclopedia Press. Pyoungyang.

Kim, S.K., Kim, K.K., Paek, K.H., Chang, W.J., Seo, K.T., 1985. Pyongyang Bukun Cave excavation report. Excavation Report Series 14, Pyongyang. In: Han, C.K. (Ed.), Prehistoric Archaeology of North

Korea (1990). Paeksanmunhwa, Seoul, pp. 69–78.
Kim, W.Y. and K.D. Bae., 1983. Report of excavation, 1979–1983, Chongokni. Bureau of Cultural Proeprties.
Kim, W.Y. and Y.H. Chung. 1979. Preliminary report of Acheulean Handaxe Bifaces from the Chongokni site, Jindanhakbo, pp. 46–47.
Kim, W.Y., Bae, K.D., 1983. Report of Excavation, 1979–1983, Chongokni. Bureau of Cultural Properties, Korea.
Kim, Y.H., Lee, H.J., Chun, S.S., Han, S.J., Chough, S.K., 1999. Holocene transgressive stratigraphy of a macrotidal flat in the southeastern Yellow Sea: Gomso Bay, Korea. Journal of Sedimentary Research 69, pp. 328–337.
Klein, R.G., 1999. The Human Career: Human Biological and Cultural Origins, seconded. University of Chicago Press, Chicago and London.
Kleindienst, M.R., 1961. Variability within the Late Acheulian assemblage in East Africa. S. Afr. Archaeol. Bull. 16, pp. 35–52.
Kuzmin, Y.V., 2007. Geoarchaeological aspects of the origin and spread of microblade technology in Northern and Central Asia. In: Kuzmin, Y.V., Keates, S.G., Shen, C. (Eds.), Origin and Spread of Microblade Technology in Northern Asia and North America. Archaeology Press, Simon Frazer University, Burnaby, BC, pp. 115–124.
Kuzmin, Y.V., Glascock, M.D., Sato, H., 2002. Sources of archaeological obsidian on Sakhalin Island (Russian Far East). Journal of Archaeological Science 29, pp. 741–749.
Lab of Human Evolution, 1995a. Cave Sites in Northwest Chosun(Korea). Kimilsung University Press. Pyoungyang.
Lab of Human Evolution, 1995b. Younggok Cave site. Kimilsung University Press. Pyoungyang.
Laboratory of Human Evolution, 1995. Cave Sites in Northwestern Korea. Kim Ilsung University Press, Pyongyang.
Larick, R., Ciochon, R.L., 1996. The African emergence and early Asian dispersals of the genus Homo. Am. Sci. 84, pp. 538–551.

Lbova, L.V., 2008. Problems of dating of the early Upper Paleolithic in the Transbaikal region. In: Derevianko, A.P., Shunkov, M.V. (Eds.), The Current Issues of Paleolithic Studies in Asia. Proceeding of the International Symposium, Asian Paleolithic Association. Publishing Department of the Institute of Archaeology and Ethnography, Novosibirsk, pp. 78-82.

Leakey, M.D., 1971. Olduvai Gorge, vol. 3. Cambridge University Press, Cambridge.

Lee, G.K., 2002. Hwasun Dosan Site. Chosun University Museum, Gwangju.

Lee, G.K., 2004. Sinbuk Upper Paleolithic Site, Jangheung County, Jollanam Province, Korea. In: Lee, G.K. (Ed.), Evaluating the Cultural Features of the Sinbuk Upper Paleolithic Site in the Northeastern Asia. Jangheung County and Chosun University Museum, Gwangju, pp. 31-38.

Lee, G.K., Kim, E.J., 2009. Preliminary report on the third excavation of Dosan site in Hwasun county. The 10th Conference of Korean Paleolithic Society, Mokpo, pp. 119-30.

Lee, G.K., Kim, M.J., 2008. Absolute chronology of Sinbuk Upper Palaeolithic site in Southwestern Korea by calibrating radiocarbon dates with CalPal 2007 Hulu curve. Journal of Honam Archaeological Society 29, pp. 5-24.

Lee, H.J., 2002a. Evolution of Paleolithic Technology in the Korean Peninsula, Paleolithic Culture in Korea. Yonsei University Press, Seoul.

Lee, H.J., 2002b. Preliminary report of the Dangga Paleolithis site, Naju, Korea, In: K. D. Bae & J. C. Lee (Eds.), Paleolithic Archaeology in Northeast Asia. Yeoncheon County & The Institute of Cultural Properties, Hanyang University. Seoul, pp. 173-180.

Lee, H.J., 2005. The Middle Paleolithic to Upper Paleolithic transition and the tradition of flake tool manufacturing on the Korean peninsula. In:

Derevianko, A.P. (Ed.), The Middle to Upper Paleolithic Transition in Eurasia, Hypothesis and Facts. Institute of Archaeology and Ethnography Press, Novosibirsk, pp. 486–500.

Lee, H.J., J.B. Kim, C.W. Chung, H.S. Im, H.Y. Lee, A.P. Derevianko, M.I. Deregacheva and N.S. Bolikhovskaya, 2006. The Paleolithic Archaeology and Quaternary Geology in the Yongsan river region. Hakyeon Press. Seoul.

Lee, H.J., J.B. Kim, J.Y.Kim, D.Y. Yang, M.Y.Hong and H.Y. Lee, 2003. New Paleolithic finds in the Lower basin of the Youngsan river, Journal of Korean Paleolithic Archaeology Society 8, pp. 67–98.

Lee, J.C. (Eds.), Paleolithic Archaeology in Northeast Asia. Yeoncheon County and The Institute of Cultural Properties, Seoul & Yeoncheon County, pp. 55–65.

Lee, K.E., 2007. Surface water changes recorded in Late Quaternary marine sediments of the Ulleung Basin, East Sea (Japan Sea). Palaeogeography, Palaeoclimatology, Palaeoecology 247, pp. 18–31.

Lee, K.G., 2004. Sinbuk Upper Paleolithic Site, Jangheung County, Jollanam Province, Korea. In: Lee, K.G. (Ed.), Evaluating the Cultural Features of the Sinbuk Upper

Leng, J., Shannon, C.L., 2000. Rethinking early Paleolithic typologies in China and India. J. East Asian Archaeol. 2, pp. 9–15.

Li, C.R., 2002. The Handaxes unearthed in China, In: (K. D. Bae & J. C. Lee, Eds.) Paleolithic Archaeology in Northeast Asia. Yeoncheon County & the Institute of Cultural Properties. Seoul. pp. 29–39.

Li, C.R., 2007. Paleolithic culture at Danjiang Reservoir in Hubei Province, China. In: Matsufuji, K. (Ed.), Environmental Change and Paleolithic Chronology in East Asia. Doshisa University, Japan, pp. 127–133.

Li, C. 2008. The culture of the Paleolithic at Danjiang Reservoir in China. In: Basic Studies of the Paleolithic Chronology and Paleoenvironmental Changes in East Asia. Kyoto, pp. 165–173

Lu, H., Zhang, H., Wang, S., Cosgrove, R., Zhao, C., Stevens, T., Zhao, J., 2007. A preliminary survey on loess deposit in Eastern Qinling Mountains (Central China) and its implication for estimating age of the Pleistocene lithic artifacts. Quatern. Sci. 27 (4). (in Chinese).

Luchterhand, K., 1978. Late Cenozoic climate, mammalian evolutionary patterns and middle Pleistocene human adaptation in Eastern Asia. In: Freeman, L.G. (Ed.), Views of the Past. Mouton, The Hague, pp. 363-421.

Lycett, S.J., 2007a. Why is there a lack of Mode 3 Levallois technologies in East Asia? a phylogenetic test of the Movius-Schick hypothesis. J. Anthropol. Archaeol. 26, pp. 541-575.

Lycett, S.J., 2007b. Is the Soanian techno-complex a Mode 1 or Mode 3 phenomenon? a morphometric assessment. J. Archaeol. Sci. 34, pp. 1434-1440.

Lycett, S.J., Bae, C.J., 2010. The Movius Line and Old World Palaeolithic patterns: the state of the debate. World Archaeology 42 (4), pp. 521-544.

Lycett, S.J., Norton, C.J., 2010. A demographic model for Palaeolithic technological evolution: the case of East Asia and the Movius Line. Quaternary International 211, pp. 55-65.

Lycett, S.J., von Cramon-Taubadel, N., 2008. Acheulean variability and hominin dispersals: a model-bound approach. J. Archaeol. Sci. 35, pp. 553-562.

Machida, H., 1999. Quaternary widespread tephra catalog in and around Japan : recent progress. Quaternary Research 38, pp. 194-201.

Madsen, D.B., Li, J., Brantingham, P.J., Gao, X., Elston, R.G., Bettinger, R.L., 2001. Dating Shuidonggou and the Upper Palaeolithic blade industry in North China. Antiquity 75 (290), pp. 706-716.

Marean, C.W., Kim, S.Y., 1998. Mousterian large-mammal remains from Kobeh Cave. Current Anthropology 39, pp. 79-113.

Matsufuji, K. K.Bae, T. Danhara, T. Naruse, A. Hayashida, K.Yu, N.

Inoue and S. Hwang, 2005. New Progress of Studies at the Chongokni Paleolithic Site, Korea: Korea _Japan cooperative Project in 2001-2004, Paleolithic Archaeology 66, pp. 1-16.

Matsufuji, K., 2003. Origin of the Upper Paleolithic in Northeast Asia, in: Bae, K.D. (Ed.), Geological Formation of the Chongokni Paleolithic Site and Paleolithic Archaeology in East Asia. Paper presented in International Seminar for Commemorating the Chongokni Site. The Institute of Cultural Properties, Hanyang University, Ansan, pp. 63-87.

Matsufuji, K., 2004. Hakuhen-sentoki and the neighbors ?people with stemmed points crossed over the Tsushima channel. In: Yi, Y.J., Ambiru, M. (Eds.), Suyanggae and Her Neighbors. The 9th International Symposium. Meiji University Museum, Tokyo, pp. 203-208.

Matsufuji, K., Okamura, M., 1998. Archaeology of Paleolithic Age (Japanese).Symposium Japanese Archaeology I, Gakusheisha, Tokyo.

McBrearty, S., Brooks, A.S., 2000. The revolution that wasn't: a new interpretation of the origin of modern human behavior. Journal of Human Evolution 39, pp. 453-563.

McDougall, I., Brown, F.H., Fleagle, J.G., 2005. Stratigraphic placement and age of modern humans from Kibish, Ethiopia. Nature 433, pp. 733-736.

McPherron, S.P., 2000. Handaxes as a measure of the mental capabilities of early hominids. J. Archaeol. Sci. 27, pp. 655-663.

Mellars, P., 1998. The Upper Paleolithic revolution. In: Cunliffe, B. (Ed.), Prehistoric Europe. Oxford University Press, Oxford, pp. 42-78.

Mellars, P., Boyle, K., Bar-Yosef, O., Stringer, C. (Eds.), 2007. Rethinking the Human Revolution: New Behavioural and Biological Perspectives on the Origin and Dispersal of Modern Humans. McDonald Institute Monographs. McDonald Institute for Archaeological Research, Cambridge.

Minoura, K., Hoshino, K., Nakamura, T., Wada, E., 1997. Late PleistoceneeHolocene paleoproductivity circulation in the Japan Sea: sea-level control on d13C and d15N records of sediment organic material. Palaeogeography, Palaeoclimatology, Palaeoecology 135, pp. 41-50.

Misra, V.N., 1987. Middle Pleistocene adaptations in India. In: Soffer, O. (Ed.), The Pleistocene Old World e Regional Perspectives. Plenum Press, New York, pp. 99-119.

Misra, V.N., 1989. Stone Age India: an ecological perspective. Man Environ. 14, pp. 17-64.

Movius, H.L., 1944. Early Man and Pleistocene Stratigraphy in Southern and Eastern Asia. Papers of the Peabody Museum of American Archaeology and Ethnology, vol. 19(3). Harvard University, Cambridge.

Movius, H.L., 1948. The Lower Paleolithic cultures of southern and eastern Asia. Trans. Am. Phil. Soc. 38, pp. 329-420.

Movius, H.L., 1956. New Palaeolithic sites, near Ting-Ts'un in the Fen river, Shansi province, North China. Quarteraria 3, pp. 13-26.

Movius, H.L., 1969. Lower Paleolithic archaeology in southern Asia and the Far East. In: Howells, W.W. (Ed.), Early Man in the Far East, Studies in Physical Anthropology No.1. Humanities Press, New York, pp. 17-82.

Movius, H.L., 1978. Southern and eastern Asia: conclusion. In: Ikawa-Smith, F. (Ed.), Early Paleolithic in South and East Asia. Mouton, The Hague, pp. 351-355.

Narue, T., M. Kazuto, H.J. Lee, T. Danhara, A. Hayashida, C.B. Kim, K.M. Yu, K. Yata and S.H. Hwang, and K. Ikeda., 2006. Preliminary Report of the loess-Paleozol stratigraphy in the Jangdongni site, Korea. In: Lee, H. J., J. B. Kim, C. W. Chung, H. S. Im, H. Y. Lee, A. P. Derevianko, M. I. Deregachevaand N. S. Bolikhovskaya(Eds.), The Paleolithic Archaeology and Quaternary Geology in the Yongsan river region, Hakyeon Publising co., Seoul, pp. 269-290.

Naruse, T., K.Bae, K. Yu, M. Kazuto, T. Danhara, A. Hayashita, S. Hwang, J. Kim and J. Shin, 2003. Loess ?Paleosol sequence in the Chongokni Paleolithic site. In: K. D. Bae & J. C. Lee (Eds.), Geological Formation of the Chongokni site and Paleolithic Archaeology in East Asia. Yeonchon County and Institute of Cultural Properties, Hanyang University, Seoul, pp. 143-156.

Naruse, T., Yu, K.M., Wantanabe, M., 2008. Loess-paleosol stratigrapht and chronology after 900 ka for constructing the Paleolithic chronology in East Asia. In: Basic Studies of the Paleolithic Chronology and Paleoenvironmental Changes in East Asia. Kyoto, pp. 65-85.

Noll, M., Petraglia, M.D., 2003. Acheulean bifaces and early human behavioral patterns in East Africa and South India. In: Soressi, M., Dibble, H.L. (Eds.), Multiple Approaches to the Study of Bifacial Technologies. University of Pennsylvania Press, Philadelphia, pp. 31-43.

Norton, C. J., 2000. The current state of Korean paleoanthropology. Journal of Human Evolution 38, pp. 803-825.

Norton, C.J., 2007. Sedentism, territorial circumscription, and the increased use of plant domesticates across Neolithic?Bronze Age Korea. Asian Perspectives 46(1), pp. 133-165.

Norton, C and K. Bae, 2005. Middle Pleistocene Handaxes the Korean Peninsula, Journal of Human Evolution.

Norton, C.J., Bae, K., Harris, J.W.K., Lee, H., 2006. Middle Pleistocene handaxes from the Korean Peninsula. J. Hum. Evol. 51, pp. 527-536.

Norton, C.J., Bae, K.D., 2009. Erratum to "The Movius Line sensu lato (Norton et al., 2006) further assessed and defined" J. H. Evol. 55 (2008) 1148-1150. Journal of Human Evolution 57, pp. 331-334.

Norton, C.J., Bae, K.D., Harris, J.W.K., Lee, H.Y., 2006. Middle Pleistocene handaxes from the Korean Peninsula. Journal of Human Evolution 51, pp. 527-536.

Norton, C.J., Bae, K.D., Lee, H.Y., Harris, J.W.K., 2007. A review of Korean microlithic industries. In: Keates, S., Kuzmin, Y., Shen, C. (Eds.), Origin and Spread of Microblade Technology in Northern Asia and North America. Archaeology Press, Vancouver, pp. 91-102.

Norton, C.J., Gao, X., 2008a. Hominin-carnivore interactions during the Chinese Early Paleolithic: taphonomic perspectives from Xujiayao. Journal of Human Evolution 55, pp. 164-178.

Norton, C.J., Gao, X., 2008b. Zhoukoudian Upper Cave revisited: a taphonomic perspective. Current Anthropology 49, pp. 732-745.

Norton, C.J., Gao, X., Feng, X.W., 2009. The criteria defining the East Asian Middle Paleolithic reexamined. In: Camps, M., Chauhan, P.R. (Eds.), Sourcebook of Paleolithic Transitions: Methods, Theories, and Interpretations. Springer Press, Dordrecht, The Netherlands, pp. 245-254.

Norton, C.J., Hasegawa, Y., Kohno, N., Tomida, Y., 2007b. Distinguishing archaeological and paleontological faunal collections from Pleistocene Japan: taphonomic perspectives from Hanaizumi. Anthropological Science 115, pp. 91-106.

Norton, C.J., Jin, C.Z.,Wang, Y., Zhang, Y.Q., 2010b. Rethinking the Palearctic-Oriental biogeographic boundary in Quaternary China. In: Norton, C.J., Braun, D. (Eds.), Asian Paleoanthropology: From Africa to China and Beyond. Vertebrate Paleobiology and Paleoanthropology Series. Springer Press, Dordrecht, The Netherlands, pp. 81-100.

Norton, C.J., Jin, J., 2009. The evolution of modern humans in East Asia: behavioral perspectives. Evolutionary Anthropology 18, pp. 247-260.

Norton, C.J., Kondo, Y., Ono, A., Zhang, Y.Q., Diab, M., 2010a. The nature of megafaunal extinctions during the MIS 3e2 transition in Japan. Quaternary International 211, pp. 113-122.

Norton. C.J., K. Bae, J.W.K Harris and H. Lee, 2006. Middle Pleistocene handaxes from the Korean Peninsula, J. of Human Evolution 51. pp. 527-536.

Obata, H., 2003. Early stage of Upper Paleolithic Age in the Korean Peninsula, in: Inada. In: Searching for the Beginning of the Upper Paleolithic in Japan. Japanese Paleolithic Research Association, Yokohama, pp. 80-96.

Olsen, J.W., Miller-Antonio, S., 1992. The Palaeolithic in southern China. Asian Perspect. 31, pp. 129-160.

Otte, M., Kozlowski, J.K., 2005. The transition from the Middle to Upper Paleolithic in North Eurasia. In: Derevianko, A.P. (Ed.), The Middle to Upper Paleolithic Transition in Eurasia, Hypothesis and Facts. Institute of Archaeology and Ethnography Press, Novosibirsk, pp. 20-31.

Paddayya, K., Blackwell, B.A.B., Jhaldiyal, R., Petraglia, M.D., Fevrier, S.,Chaderton II, D.A., Blickstein, J.I.B., Skinner, A.R., 2002. Recent findings on the Acheulian of the Hunsgi and Baichbal valleys, Karnataka, with special reference to the Isampur excavation and its dating. Curr. Sci. 83, pp. 641-647.

Paddayya, K., Petraglia, M.D., 1993. Formation processes of Acheulean localities in the Hunsgi and Baichbal Valleys, Peninsular India. In: Goldberg, P.,Nash, D.T., Petraglia, M.D. (Eds.), Formation Processes in Archaeological Context. Prehistory Press, Madison, pp. 61-82.

Paleolithic Site in the Northeastern Asia. Jangheung County and Chosun University Museum, Gwangju, pp. 31-38.

Park, J.H. and D.K. Hong, 2007. OSL dates of the Mansuri site, Cheongwon, Proceedings of Prehistoric Seminar of the Mansuri Paleolithic Site, Cheongwon, pp. 78-85.

Park, S.J. and E.K. Lee, 2004. Fossil men in Korea, Journal of Korean Paleolithic Archaeology Society 7, pp. 41-51.

Park, S.J., 1992. The Pleistocene hominid fossils in Korea. In: Sohn, P.K. (Ed.), KoreaeChina QuaternaryePrehistory Symposium. Korea Anthropological Institute, Dankook University, Seoul, pp. 112-114.

Park, S.J., Lee, E.K., 2003. Fossil men in Korea. Journal of Korean

Paleolithic Archaeology 7, pp. 41–51.
Park, S.J., Lee, Y.J., 1990. A new discovery of the Upper Pleistocene child's skeleton from Hungsu Cave (Turubong Cave Complex) Ch'ongwon, Korea. Korean Journal of Quaternary Research 4, pp. 1–14.
Park, Y.A., 1994. The sea level and coastal shoreline of the early and middle Holocene in the Yellow Sea. In: Kim, B.M., Bae, K.D. (Eds.), Environment and Culture in the Yellow Sea Region. Hakyounmunhwasa, Seoul, pp. 7–13.
Park, Y.A., 2001. Korean Quaternary Environment. Seoul National University Press, Seoul.
Pei, W.C., Woo, J.K., Chia, L.P., Chow, M.C., Liu, H.T., Wang, C.Y., 1958. Report on the Excavation of Palaeolithic Sites at Tingtsun, Hsiangfenhsien, Shansi Province, China. Science Press, Beijing.
Petraglia, M.D., 1998. The Lower Paleolithic of India and its bearing on the Asian record. In: Petraglia, M.D., Korisettar, R. (Eds.), Early Human Behaviour in Global Context: The Rise and Diversity of the Lower Palaeolithic Record. Routledge Press, London, pp. 343–390.
Petraglia, M.D., 2005. Hominin responses to Pleistocene environmental change in Arabia and South Asia. In: Head, M.J., Gibbard, P.L. (Eds.), Early–Middle Pleistocene Transitions: The LandeOcean Evidence. Geological Society, London. Special Publications 247.
Petraglia, M.D., Shipton, C., 2008. Large cutting tool variation west and east of the Movius Line. J. Hum. Evol. 55, pp. 962–966.
Pope, G.G., 1989. Bamboo and human evolution. Nat. Hist. 10, pp. 48–57.
Pope, G.G., Keates, S.G., 1994. The evolution of human cognition and cultural capacity. In: Corruccini, R.S., Ciochon, R.L. (Eds.), Integrative Paths to the Past. Prentice Hall, Englewood Cliffs, NJ, pp. 531–567.
Potts, R., 1988. Early Hominid Activity at Olduvai Gorge. Aldine de Gruyter, New York. pp. 225–241.
Qiu, Z.L., 1985. The Middle Palaeolithic of China. In: Wu, R.K., Olsen,

J.W. (Eds.), Palaeoanthropology and Palaeolithic Archaeology in the People's Republic of China. Academic Press, Orlando, pp. 187–210.

Richards, M.P., Pettitt, P.B., Trinkaus, E., Smith, F.H., Paunovic, M., Karavanic, I., 2000. Neanderthal diet at Vindija and Neanderthal predation: the evidence from stable isotopes. Proceedings of the National Academy of Sciences USA 97, pp. 663–666.

Roe, D.A., 1964. The British Lower and Middle Paleolithic: some problems, methods of study and preliminary results. Proc. Prehisty. Soc. 30, pp. 245–267.

Roe, D.A., 1968. British Lower and Middle Paleolithic handaxe groups. Proc. Prehist. Soc. 34, pp. 1–82.

Roe, D.A., 1981. The Lower and Middle Palaeolithic Periods in Britain. Routledge, London.

Roe, D.A., 1994. A metrical analysis of selected sets of handaxes and cleavers from Olduvai Gorge. In: Leakey, M.D., Roe, D.A. (Eds.), Olduvai Gorge, vol. 5. Cambridge University Press, Cambridge, pp. 146–234.

Sato, H., 2008. Human ecosystem changes in the northern circum Japan Sea in Late Pleistocene. In: Sato, H. (Ed.), International Symposium on Human Ecosystem Changes in the Northern Circum Japan Sea Area (NCJSA) in Late Pleistocene. Archaeology Laboratory, Graduate School, Tokyo University, Tokyo, pp. 2–18.

Sato, H., Tsutsumi, T., 2007. The Japanese microblade industries; technology, raw material procurement, and adaptations. In: Kuzmin, Y.V., Keates, S.G., Shen, C.(Eds.), Origin and Spread of Microblade Technology in Northern Asia and North America. Archaeology Press, Simon Fraser University, Burnaby, Canada, pp. 53–78.

Schick, K.D., 1994. The Movius Line reconsidered. In: Corruccini, R.S., Ciochon, R.L. (Eds.), Integrative Paths to the Past. Prentice Hall, Englewood Cliffs, NJ, pp. 569–596.

Schick, K.D., Dong, Z., 1993. Early Paleolithic of China and Eastern Asia.

Evol. Anthropol. 2, pp. 22-35.
Schick, K.D., Toth, N., 1993. Making Silent Stones Speak: Human Evolution and the Dawn of Technology. Simon and Schuster, New York.
Schick, K.D., Toth, N., 2001. Paleoanthropology at the millennium. In: Feinman, G.M., Price, T.D. (Eds.), Archaeology at the Millennium: A Sourcebook. Kluwer Academic/Plenum, New York, pp. 39-108.
Seo, K.T., 1987. Stone industry from the Mandal cave site. Joseongogoyongu (Archaeological Studies in Chosun) 87 (2), pp. 15-24.
Seo, Y.N., Kim, H.J., Chang, Y.J., 1999. Upper Paleolithic culture from the Koryeri site, Milyang, in: Paleolithic Sites in Youngnam Area. Proceedings of the Youngnam Archaeological Society. The Youngnam Archaeological Society, Daegu, pp. 65-82.
Seong, C.T., 2006a. A comparative and evolutionary approach to the Korean Paleolithic assemblages. Journal of Korean Ancient Historical Society 51, pp. 5-42.
Seong, C.T., 2006b. Structure and evolution of late Paleolithic assemblages in Korea. Journal of the Korean Archaeological Society 59, pp. 4-39.
Seong, C.T., 2007. Late Pleistocene microlithic assemblages in Korea. In: Kuzmin, Y.V., Keates, S.G., Shen, C. (Eds.), Origin and Spread of Microblade Technology in Northern Asia and North America. Archaeology Press, Simon Fraser University, Burnaby, B.C, pp. 103-114.
Seong, C.T., 2008. Tanged points, microblades and Late Palaeolithic hunting in Korea. Antiquity 82, pp. 871-883.
Seong, C.T., 2009. Emergence of a blade industry and evolution of Late Paleolithic technology in the Republic of Korea. Journal of Anthropological Research 65, pp. 417-451.
Shang, H., Tong, H., Zhang, S., Chen, F., Trinkaus, E., 2007. An early

modern human from Tianyuan Cave, Zhoukoudian, China. Proceedings of the National Academy of Sciences (USA) 104, pp. 573-578.

Shea, J.J., 2006. The origins of lithic projectile point technology: evidence from Africa, the Levant, and Europe. Journal of Archaeological Science 33, 823-846.

Shea, J.J., 2007. Lithic archaeology, or what stone tools can (and can't) tell us about early hominin diet. In: Ungar, P.S. (Ed.), Evolution of the Human Diet. Oxford University Press, New York, pp. 212-232.

Shea, J.J., 2011.Homosapiens is asHomosapienswas. Current Anthropology 52,1-35.

Shen, G.J., Ku, T.L., Cheng, H., Edwards, R.L., Yuan, Z.X., Wang, Q., 2001. Highprecision U-series dating of Locality 1 at Zhoukoudian, China. J. Hum. Evol. 41, pp. 676-688.

Shi, H., Dong, Y.L., Wen, B., Xiao, C.J., Underhill, P.A., Shen, P.D., Chakraborty, R., Jin, L., Su, B., 2005. Y-chromosome evidence of southern origin of the East Asian-specific haplogroup O3-M122. American Journal of Human Genetics 77, pp. 408-419.

Shi, H., Zhong, H., Peng, Y., Dong, Y.L., Qi, X.B., Zhang, F., Liu, L.F., Tan, S.J., Ma, R.Z., Xiao, C.J., Wells, R.S., Jin, L., Su, B., 2008. Y chromosome evidence of earliest modern human settlement in East Asia and multiple origins of Tibetan and Japanese populations. BioMedCentral Biology 6, p. 45.

Shimelmitz, R., Barkai, R., Gopher, A., 2011. Systematic blade production at late Lower Paleolithic (400-200 kyr) Qesem Cave, Israel. Journal of Human Evolution 61, pp. 458-479.

Sohn, P.K., 1967. Stratified Sokchangni Paleolithic site. Ryoksahakbo (Korean Historical Review) 35/36, 1-25.

Sohn, P. K., 1972. Lower and Middle Paleolithic Cultural Layers at the Sokchangni site, Hankuksayongu (Study of Korean History) 7, pp. 1-58.

Sohn, P.K., 1978. The early Paleolithic industries of Sokchangni, Korea.

In: Ikawa-Smith, F. (Ed.), Early Paleolithic in South and East Asia. Mouton, Hague and Paris, pp. 233-245.

Sohn, P. K., 1985. Report of excavation of the Dodam Keumgul site, Report of extended excavations in the Chungju Dam construction area. Chungbuk University Museum. Chongju, pp. 1-110.

Sohn, P. K., 1988. Guidebook of Study of Paleolithic Archaeology in Korea. Yonsei University Press.

Sohn, P. K., 1990. Paleolithic site in Korea and Manchuria. Korean Institute of Prehistory. Seoul.

Sohn, P. K., 1993. Sokchangni Prehistoric Site (Sokchangni Sonsa Yujok). Dong A press. Seoul.

Sohn, P. K. et. al. 2002. Paleolithic Culture in Korea. Yonsei University Press. Seoul.

Stoneking, M., Delfin, F., 2010. The human genetic history of East Asia: weaving a complex tapestry. Current Biology 20, pp. 188-193.

Su, B., Xiao, J., Underhill, P., Deka, R., Zhang, W., Akey, J., Huang, W., Shen, D., Lu, D. Chu, J., Tan, J., Shen, P., Davis, R., Cavalli-Sforza, L.L., Chakraborty, R., Xiong, M.,Du, R., Oefner, P., Chen, Z., Jin, L., 1999. Y-chromosome evidence for a northward migration of modern humans into Eastern Asia during the last Ice Age. American Journal of Human Genetics 65, 1718-1724.

Toth, N., Schick, K.D., 2009. African origins. In: Scarre, C. (Ed.), The Human Past, second ed. Thames & Hudson, London, pp. 46-83.

Toth, N., Schick, K.D., 1986. The first million yeas: the archaeology of protohuman culture. Adv. Archaeol. Meth. Theor. 9, pp. 1-96.

Villa, P., 2001. Early Italy and the colonization of Western Europe. Quatern. Int. 75, 113-130.

Wang, H.M., Pei, S.W., Ma, X.L., Feng, X.W., 2007. A preliminary report on the excavations of Shuidonggou localities 3,4,5 in Ningxia. Acta Anthropologica Sinica 26 (3), pp. 206-221.

Wang, S.J., 2005. Perspectives on Hominid Behaviour and Settlement

Patterns: a Study of the Lower Palaeolithic Sites in the Luonan Basin, China. Archaeopress, Oxford.

Wang, S.J., 2007. The Paleolithic Open-air Sites in the Luonan Basin, China. Shaanxi Provincial Institute of Archaeology, Cultural Relics Administrative Committee of Shangluo District, Museum of Luonan County. Science Press, Beijing (in Chinese).

Wang, S.J., Cosgrove, R., Lu, H.Y., Shen, C., 2007. New progress on Palaeolithic archaeological studies south in the Luohe river valley, China. In: Matsufuji, K. (Ed.), Environmental Change and Paleolithic Chronology in East Asia. Doshisa University, Japan, pp. 134-139.

Wang, Y.P., 1997. The Pleistocene Environment and the Development of the Paleolithic Cultures in South China. Beijing University Press, Beijing.

Wang, Y.P., 2004. The Upper Paleolithic in China. In: Lee, G.K. (Ed.), Evaluating the Cultural Features of the Sinbuk Upper Paleolithic Site in the Northeastern Asia.

Wang, S,J., Consgrove, R., Lu, H.Y., Shen, C., Wei M., Zheng, X.B., 2008. New Progress on Paleolithic Archaeological Studies in the Luonan Basin, Eastern Qinling Mountains, Chaina. In: Basic Studies of the Paleolithic Chronology and Paleoenvironmental Changes in East Asia. Kyoto, pp. 147-163

Wu, X.Z., Poirier, F.E., 1995. Human Evolution in China. Oxford University Press, Oxford.

Wynn, T., 1995. Handaxe enigmas. World Archaeol. 27, pp. 10-24.

Wynn, T., Tierson, F., 1990. Regional comparisons of the shapes of later Acheulean handaxes. Am. Anthropol. 92, pp. 73-84.

Xue, Y., Zerjal, T., Bao, W., Zhu, S., Shu, Q., Xu, J., Du, R., Fu, S., Li, P., Hurles, M.E., Yang, H., Tyler-Smith, C., 2006. Male demography in East Asia: a north-south contrast in human population expansion times. Genetics 172, pp. 2431-2439.

Yamanaka, I., 1995. L'industrie lithique du site de

Shuidonggou(Chei-tong-kou) dans l'Ordos en Chine. Research Summary, College of Literature, N. 32. Kyoto University, Kyoto, pp. 105-114.

Yang, J.S., Hong, M.Y., Kim, J.R., Kim, N.H., Mo, H.S., Kim, J.H. (Eds.), 2008. The Deokso Site. The University of Suwon Museum, Hwaseong.

Yao, Y.G., Nie, L., Harpending, H., Fu, Y.X., Yuan, Z.G., Zhang, Y.P., 2002. Genetic relationship of Chinese ethnic populations revealed by mtDNA sequence diversity. American Journal of Physical Anthropology 118, pp. 63-76.

Y-chromosome investigation suggests post-Glacial migrations of modern humans into East Asia via the northern route. Molecular Biology and Evolution 28, pp. 717-727.

Yi, S. B., 1989. Northeast Asian Paleolithic Research. Seoul: Seoul National University Press (in Korean).

Yi, S. B., 1996. On the age of the Paleolithic sites from the Imjingang Basin. Journal of the Korean Archaeological Society 34, pp. 135-159 (in Korean).

Yi, S.B., 2001. Middle and Upper Paleolithic transition in Korea; a brief review. Journal of the Korean Paleolithic Society 4, pp. 17-24.

Yi, S. B. 2002. Preliminary report of the Jangsani site- Paleolithic site of the Lower or early Middle Pleistocen.)Paleolithic Archaeology in Northeast Asia. Seoul, Korea: Yeoncheon County & The Institute of Cultural Properties, Hanyang University.

Yi, S.B., Arai, F., Soda, T., 1998. New discovery of Aira-Tn Ash (AT) in Korea. J. Korean Geogr. Soc. 33, pp. 447-454.

Yi, S.B., Clark, G.A., 1983. Observations on the Lower Palaeolithic of Northeast Asia. Curr. Anthropol. 24, pp. 181-202.

Yi, S.B., Lee, K.D., 1993. Chuwoli and Kawoli Paleolithic Sites, Imjin River Basin, Korea. Seoul National University Press, Seoul (in Korean).

Yi, Y.J., 1984. Excavation report on Danyang Suyanggae Paleolithic site. In: Chungbuk National University Museum (Ed.), Excavation Report on Cultural Sites in Districts Submerged due to Chungju Dam. Chungbuk National University Museum, Cheongju, pp. 101–186.

Yi, Y.J., 2007. Overview of the Excavation of the Mansuri Paleolithic Site, Proceedings of Prehistoric Seminar of the Mansuri Paleolithic Site, Cheongwon, pp. 13–43.

Yi, Y.J. and M.Y. Hong. 1999. Preliminary report of the excavation of the Bongmyoungdong Paleolithic site, Annual Review 8, The Chungbuk National University Museum, pp. 103–112.

Yi, Y.J. and S.J. Kong, 2004. Paleolithic Culture of the Songduri site, Jinchon, Korea, Paleolithic Archaeology in Korea 10, pp. 47–49.

Yi, Y.J., Wu, J.Y., Kong, S.J., 1999. A study of tang point from the Suyanggae site. In: Yi, Y.J. (Ed.), Suyanggae and Her Neighbors. The 4th International Symposium. Chungbuk University Museum and Regional Association of Tanyang History Study, Cheongju.

Yoo, Y. W., 1997. A study on the Palaeolithic industry of Imjin–Hantan Riverine area: featuring handaxes. M.A. Thesis, Seoul National University (in Korean).

Yoo, Y. w., 2007. Long–term Changes in the Organization of Lithic Technology: A Case Study from the Imjin–Hantan River Area, Korea. Ph.D. Dissertation, McGill University, Montreal.

Zhang, S., Pei, W., 1985. A Study on the Lithic Artifacts of Sinanthropus. Science Press, Beijing.